FORM,
SPACE,
AND VISION

FORM,
SPACE,
AND VISION
discovering design through drawing

GRAHAM COLLIER

Foreword by SIR HERBERT READ

PRENTICE-HALL, INC., Englewood Cliffs, N. J.

PRENTICE-HALL INTERNATIONAL, INC., *London*
PRENTICE-HALL OF AUSTRALIA, PTY., LTD., *Sydney*
PRENTICE-HALL OF CANADA, LTD., *Toronto*
PRENTICE-HALL FRANCE, S.A.R.L., *Paris*
PRENTICE-HALL OF JAPAN, INC., *Tokyo*
PRENTICE-HALL DE MEXICO, S.A., *Mexico City*

Dedicated to my children

WENDY,

RUTH,

and ANDREW

foreword

I am often asked if it is possible to teach "modern art"—by which the questioner means whether there is a short cut to skill or efficiency in such contemporary styles as the abstract or non-figurative. My first inclination is to evade the question—I do not like being responsible for other people's destinies. But if I am compelled to answer, I murmur something about "contact with things," "immersion in physical materials," "the discipline of the senses." Go to the potter's wheel, I have sometimes said, and when you can throw a bowl with a perfect outline, you will be ready to indulge in action painting. Spontaneity is not enough—or, to be more exact, spontaneity is not possible until there is an unconscious coordination of form, space, and vision.

These are the three elements which Mr. Collier has chosen as the prime concern of the teacher of art; and, good teacher that he is, he knows that the nature of these elements cannot be realized conceptually, but must be discovered experimentally. This is a book of "exercises," and is not only clear and practical, as every manual must be, but is throughout informed by the author's awareness of the limits of art and of the dangers of dogmatism. He knows also that art involves imagination as well as skill, and that even imagination cannot be left to chance, but has laws of its own origination, as Coleridge called them. It will be said that imagination is a gift and cannot be taught—turn then to Part Two of this book and you will find such a superstition refuted. This is the most original contribution that Mr. Collier has made to the teaching of art, and I know of no previous treatise that has dared to define the laws of visual imagination, and to build an educational method on them.

Mr. Collier is not unknown to me. For a few years we were neighbors in England and I had an opportunity then of observing the inspiring character of his teaching. We have lost his physical presence in our schools, but I am happy to find that he can express himself so clearly that teachers everywhere can now adopt and adapt his methods to the needs of their pupils. This is an illuminating book and will help even the general reader to a better understanding of art.

HERBERT READ

preface

A book owes its origin to many influences experienced from many different sources that have affected its author. The years past are, in many ways perhaps, more important than the present, for the formative influences necessarily lie behind us. I must, consequently, admit my debt to those special among my friends in England who have enlarged my understanding of the phenomena of art, while at the same time acknowledging the encouragement and opportunity to write this book afforded me in the United States.

I remember many searching, stimulating conversations at Lancing with John Dancy, now Master of Marlborough College, pertaining to the nature of the creative impulse and its importance in education. The rare insight and sensitivity to the visual arts of my old friends and colleagues at Lancing, Roger Lockyer and Henry Thorold, helped shape much of my own attitude, while our mutual friend, the late Martin Wigg, conspired also to increase my understanding. Among painters, I must acknowledge the valuable hours spent at Fawley Bottom with John Piper, where an ineffable sensitivity to the urges of the spirit and an awareness of the sacred elements present in even the simplest things pervade the atmosphere. Among writers and philosophers, Herbert Read stands as a constant source of inspiration through both his writings and his friendship.

The drawings illustrating this text are the work of students in basic drawing courses at Western Washington State College. Individually, they are too numerous to list, but I must thank them all for allowing me to reproduce their work. The over-all standard of the drawings is reasonably good for beginning students, who have in many cases no previous experience in art, but I should mention that these illustrations were not selected with any professional standard in mind, rather for their directness and sincerity as beginners' drawings.

Photographs of some aspect of nature are to be found in almost every chapter. Some of these are my own; but many of them, and the best of them, come from the observant eye of John Albaugh.* I am grateful to him for spending so many months searching these things out and identifying himself so much with the spirit of the book. Other photographs of nature

---

* Figs. 4-3, 4-4, 4-5, 4-20, 5-1, 5-2, 5-4, 5-9, 9-1, 9-11, 11-14, 17-2.

have come from Mildred Sutherland (Fig. 8-2), and Leona Sundquist gave me a free hand with many of her fine biological photographs from which I selected two (Figs. 8-3 and 20-1). I wish to thank them both.

I must also express my appreciation to the galleries, collectors, and artists who so willingly supplied the illustrations I desired, especially to Victor Pasmore in London for allowing me to select from very recent drawings, paintings, and constructions, and to Ernest Mundt in San Francisco for affording me a similar wide selection from his sculpture.

I have made considerable use of many of my colleagues at Western Washington State College. I wish to thank particularly Dr. Arnold Lahti, Dr. Edward Neuzil, and Dr. William Bender for their help with those chapters dealing with dynamics in art; also Professor James Hildebrand for his advice on many issues that have arisen concerning the mathematical implications of form structure and dynamics. I am grateful to Dr. William Proweller for allowing me to use Review Fig. 3 and for his constant willingness to argue difficult points; and to Dr. James L. Jarrett for clarifying problems in the presentation of the subject matter. Robert Bragg has given me considerable help in making the right emphases among the many concepts argued in the text.

I am indebted to Dr. Herbert Taylor and the Research Advisory Committee of Western Washington State College for their generous help in the preparation of the manuscript, and to Jane Clark for her patient and skillful typing. I must record my thanks to Robert B. Davis for his enthusiastic support from the beginning, to the early reviewers of the material for their sympathetic reception and wise suggestions, and to that fine editor, James M. Guiher. His skillful pruning of verbosity, clarification of concepts, and empathy for the manuscript generally have played an important part in the writing. Finally, my appreciation to Maurine Lewis for her hard work in the production stages of the book, and to Marvin Warshaw for the many hours spent in designing and laying it out.

I wish to thank my wife, Mary, for her patient understanding and tolerance in leaving me so well alone to work.

GRAHAM COLLIER

contents

x

introduction

It may sound odd for the author of this book to announce at the outset that he has always been dubious about the effectiveness of a book dealing with the practice of art. Artists are engaged in an extremely complex activity. They try to express their attitudes to life through visual images—better say they experience a compulsion to do this— and it is hopelessly wrong to suggest that skills constitute the most important criterion of quality in the visual arts. Proficiency in handling materials is not proof that one is an artist.

If technical competence is not of prime importance, what should be the subject of a book concerned with the creative acts of art? Our answer in this volume is that skill is less important than awareness, that the appearance of things is less important than their meaning and aesthetic significance, and that imaginative reality is at least as important as sensory reality. The thesis is not easily explained, for words convey but poorly the mysterious power of the visual image. We are affected by shape, color, and texture, by form and space, in a way that is all but impossible to describe verbally. But the attempt must be made if we believe that art greatly enriches human experience and enlarges our world by adding a new dimension to it.

Our aim is to produce a book that is worthy of this higher

1

function of art, the function that Sir Herbert Read describes as "the mental processes which lead to the creation of the most permanent achievements of mankind. . . ."[1] Since it is our theory that the best way to understand art is to "do" it, we shall approach the subject through drawing; and through "doing," we hope to initiate a creative experience. At the same time we shall bring in broader aesthetic ideas and relate them to specific exercises, so that some understanding of the revealing function of art will also be gained. There is an unnatural tendency in higher education to separate the practice of art from the history of art—an unfortunate dichotomy and one that does not exist for any artist worthy of the name. Today, all artists are powerfully influenced by the art of the past: the artist lives with the images of art; there is a sort of mystical "laying on of hands" from the great artists in history to those of today. Providing historical perspective, references will be made throughout the text to art and architecture of the near and distant past. The concepts discussed here are essentially timeless. They are to be found in the art of differing ages, and "modern art" should be seen as evolving logically and naturally from the art of the past.

The urge to draw is instinctive in all children. They use drawing as a very personal and intimate way of making statements about memory, about desire, and about mood. Accurate representation is generally not their concern. But as children grow up in our strongly rational civilization, in our verbal culture, their early affinity for personally created images dies away, and drawing becomes associated with "commercial" art, "industrial" art, or "fine" art. The philosophy of this book is that drawing should be used by beginning students to record their personal and instinctive reactions to all kinds of stimuli, whether initiated by the senses, by the intuition, by the emotions, or by the intellect. We also maintain that drawing is the *first* means of expression; that a piece of sculpture, a work of architecture, a painting, a contemporary table lamp, more often than not, takes shape first as a drawing—hence the subtitle, *Discovering Design through Drawing*. If "design" means *bringing into being*—the visual and technical organization of a work of art—then drawing and design are inextricably linked, though

---

[1] Sir Herbert Read, *The Forms of Things Unknown* (New York: Horizon Press, 1960), p. 28.

2

we may draw without any intent to design. Rather does design grow inspirationally out of the act of drawing. "Drawing," in this context, signifies the use of any medium to mark on a drawing surface some concrete visual form embodying an idea, a feeling, or a picture in the mind.

The drawing experiments in the book will attempt to *involve* the student in a series of fundamental experiences. He will be asked to look intently at many things and to search and analyze rather than tacitly to accept. He will be confronted with many problems of form and the all-pervading element of space. After sharpening his perception, and thereby his greater understanding, of both form and space (actually we are incapable of perceiving either one separately), the reader is asked to develop an attitude or mood about them—to generate an aesthetic response to form and space, an involvement which we hope is built into every experiment. This aesthetic response can spring from two sources: from the intellect and from feeling. Both are ways of knowing and recognizing those special qualities of form and space which activate our aesthetic sensibilities. Both are required to make an adequate response, and both are called upon in these experiments.

An act of perception alone, even when acute, is insufficient to produce a work of art. There must also be the compulsive force of the imagination, for only the imagination has the power to turn fact into art. We say a person has "vision" when he combines a capacity for heightened perception with a sensitive imagination and is strongly affected by mood. Part Two of the book introduces the student to the imaginative reality of art.

The chapters of the book are conceived as a sequence of experiments, for the later work builds on the experiences of the earlier sections. But there is nothing rigid about this format; the instructor or the student can elect to complete the work dealing with form before he becomes involved with space—or vice versa—should he so desire.

The aim of this beginning work in art is to awaken the reader's visual curiosity; to give him confidence, so that he can readily express himself through drawing; to encourage him to deepen his awareness of the objects and forms around him; to sharpen his ability to respond through drawing to these forms; to induce personal attitudes, of which he becomes aware, to form and space—in summary, to increase his capacity for personal vision. All these are basic factors which are necessary for any future specialized study in art.

Everyone is capable of a creative act in the visual arts. This is manifestly true for children, but it also holds for older youths and adults, providing the unsophisticated attitude of the child can be restored, the curiosity and wonder. All people should not be measured against a Paul Klee or an Henri Matisse, but they can be held to the same standards of imagination, insight, and creativity that we expect of them in papers written in an English or philosophy course. It is our hope that this book may provide the reader with a vocabulary of art and with an insight into its workings that will enable him to place greater reliance on the creative, rather than the imitative, act of drawing. And he should gain some standards of aesthetic judgment that will help him distinguish the genuine from the fake, the natural from the contrived, art from craft.

As Max Scheler says, the purpose of art is "not to reproduce what is already given (which would be superfluous), nor to create something in the pure play of subjective fancy (which can only be transitory and must necessarily be a matter of complete indifference to other people), but to press forward into the whole of the external world *and* the soul, to see and communicate those objective realities within it which rule and convention have hitherto concealed." [2]

---

[2] Max Scheler, *The Nature of Sympathy*, trans. P. Heath (London: Routledge, 1954), p. 253.

PART ONE

form and space

We have no visual knowledge of any kind except that of form and space. The dimensions of space determine the world in which we move and live; and space, in turn, is defined by the objects or forms that occupy space. The artist, concerned with giving visual expression to his perceptions and creative imagination, cannot avoid re-creating form in space, for there can be no visual communication that is formless and spaceless—there is just nothing at all.

This seems very obvious, but it must be impressed on the reader how fundamental in art are the concepts of form and space. The practice and philosophy of art must start with them. The eleven chapters in the first half of this book are designed to involve the reader in certain aspects of form and space, and with the interrelationship between the two. The experiments are not meant to be comprehensive, but merely an introduction to two of the three basic factors underlying the whole structure of the visual arts. The third is the element we call "vision," which is the concern of Part Two.

The five aspects of form with which we shall be concerned are its structural, aesthetic, organic, tactile and dynamic qualities. Each experiment is only a starting point for further discoveries about these qualities. Involving the student in a personal awareness of space is more difficult. As you will see, space must be approached through an awareness of form. Consequently, the experiments dealing with space also involve form. The operation of forces in space, the space appraisal of the intuition, the reasoning of the mind, and the "natural" perception of the third dimension are the prime concerns of the experiments involving spatial awareness.

5

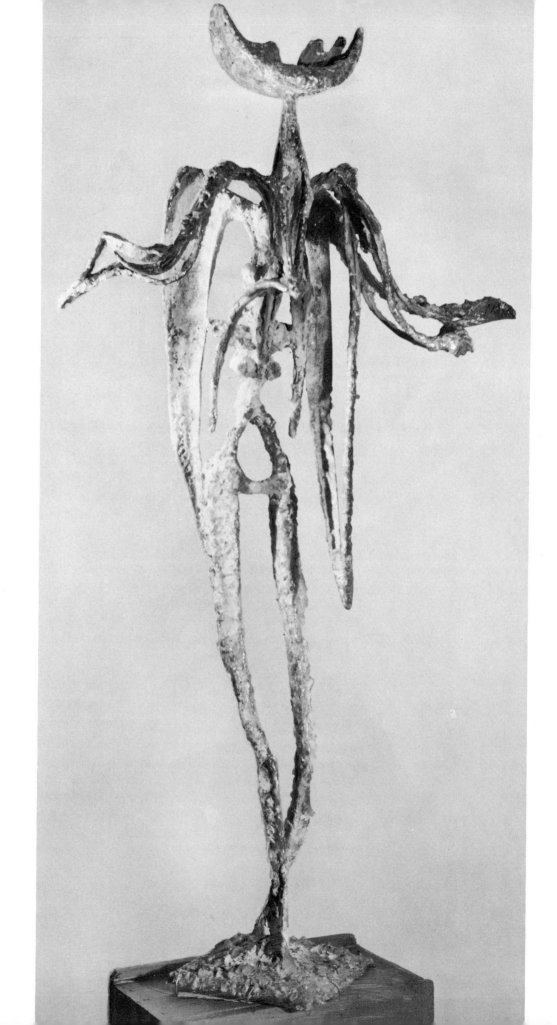

1

structural families: the skeletal object

In this first drawing experiment, our principal objectives are:

1. To train your powers of *observation* so that you can better analyze the structure of form.

2. To develop your ability to *make a drawing* on the basis of this observation and analysis.

3. To expand your *knowledge of form* through drawing of this kind.

4. To enhance your ability to see the *creative potential* in a drawing based on analysis of structure.

5. To point out that form is entirely *dependent on structure.*

These are five basic statements about drawing. If the words in italics are extracted from each statement, we can summarize the objectives in this way. Observe and analyze the object to make a drawing based on your knowledge of form, keeping an eye on the creative potential of the drawing. The final drawing should reflect the fact that form is dependent on structure. These words sum up the aims which are behind most beginning student work. They do not tell the whole story about the creative, revealing function of art, but they are the bones on which the whole body of art will grow.

Some artists would not agree that observation is crucial in

RITE OF PASSAGE
Theodore Roszak
Sculpture in steel, nickel, and copper. The figure abstracted to a skeletal form which, nevertheless, makes strong suggestions of volume and sharply defines regions of space.
(Pierre Matisse Gallery, New York. Photograph by Flair Studios)

7

the work of a mature painter or sculptor; and in the sense that we are using the word, implying a conscious looking, they would be justified. But for the student, a capacity for observation is vital. However, at any stage of development, the memory of a thing seen is a prototype image on which the artist's imagination will build. Even the nonobjective artist is immersed in the world of things seen, from which he gathers much of his knowledge of form. There are many ways of regarding an object, from a superficial glance to a penetrating scrutiny, casually and disinterestedly or with intent and involvement. When we look with intent we try to see beyond the immediate, apparent shape of the object into its true and essential structure to understand "how" it is. This will also yield understanding of "why" it is, what is its function, and what part it plays in its particular setting. It is this type of looking which enables us to see the design potential of the object and to reveal its form through a drawing. We are led to the essential, permanent nature of the object.

Obviously, external appearances do not tell the whole story about an object. Asked to describe a tomato, the average person would say that it is a small, round, and reddish object. Some might go further and describe its softness to the touch, but relatively few would cut it open and describe its internal cross section. Yet a drawing of the tomato's cross section is just as much the tomato as the round and red object. When purchasing a new automobile, few people decide to buy solely on the basis of the "looks" of the car; they want to know how it performs and perhaps how well it is built. Similarly, to make a significant drawing of any object, one should know about its structure and function as well as its external appearance.

An inquiring person is alive with all his senses, restless with curiosity, eager to know more about himself and the worlds beyond himself. He tends to regard objects much as the prospective automobile purchaser views his gleaming new model, as objects which are *his* to enjoy and to explore visually and intellectually. Then he may, through drawing, express these several attitudes to objects. Such a person tends to identify himself with the natural world and does not restrict his curiosity and interest to the comparatively few objects he calls his own, but develops an awareness of the entire range of natural phenomena. Even in the mid-twentieth century, nature is still the master designer. Poor is the man who feels attachment only to his own possessions, for the world of nature can be more intimately "possessed" than any automobile.

We can all heighten our experiences of form by learning more about the principles of structure, for structure determines the shape of form and also its functional capacity. From a structural analysis of form, we discover that the *spatial element* of an object—the space in and around the object—is very important in our total comprehension of it. There are three important aspects of our perception of form. We search out *form-structure* in order to understand how the shape we see is constructed; we give some meaning to the object when we can ally the structure and shape to *form-function;* and when we are aware of the shape of the *surrounding space,* we have a heightened perception of the significant shape of the object. And following close on our perception of form comes our inevitable aesthetic response to it.

We can learn much from children, whose continual sense of wonder about the world is so evident in their paintings and sculpture. But like many other childhood faculties, with the coming of "mature" years, this imaginative capacity disappears. Although a few of us retain it to some degree, most of us have to redevelop it before we can take a childlike delight (which is a difficult feat for an adult) in our surroundings, and thus create the conditions under which we might enjoy an aesthetic experience. For an aesthetic experience is part wonder, part recognition. We are moved to wonder when our imagination is so strongly affected that we recognize a quality of completeness that approaches perfection. Under ideal conditions this experience can approach the transcendental.

But before we can expect to look successfully "with intent," we must train ourselves in the more elementary aspects of visual analysis, in such things as proportions, directional movements, rhythms, and organic growth—to mention just a few. In so doing, we are led inevitably to the object's structure. The aim of this first experiment is to initiate you into the processes by which simple observation can grow into the greater understanding of perception and perhaps, finally, into the full imaginative significance of "vision."

THE FIRST STRUCTURE DRAWINGS

The student should now collect four or five specimens of objects with a skeletal structure: grasses, twigs, seed-head formations, leaves, the backbones of fishes, and the bony skeletons of small animals are some possibilities (Figs. 1-4, 1-5). Once engaged in the search, you will be amazed at the variety of skeletal forms at hand. In the conclusion to this chapter skeletal structure is defined as structure which "can be represented by a number of lines moving in different directions, but all must be connected to a main stem by a series of joints in what is known as an 'articulated system.'" It is form possessing a discernible skeleton.

That discernible skeleton is what we are looking for now. Our purpose is to make a strong black-line diagram that reveals how the object "holds together" through its skeletal limbs. In the case of a leaf, we are concerned with only the central skeleton, ignoring the flesh of leaf area (Fig. 1-5). A straightforward sketch representation of its appearance is not our purpose.

To make these drawings, it is best to use a black grease pencil or a broad-nibbed drawing pen and black ink. Also, it is a good thing to make some tentative line diagrams on a rough newsprint pad, in order to get to know the object before producing the finished black drawing on a good quality offset paper. To make these drawings effective, ignore secondary detail and the outlines or edges of the form: an X-ray approach is required. A glance at Figs. 1-1 to 1-3, will show how these drawings appear. In the drawing, you could make a distinction between principal and secondary skeleton lines by means of thick and thin lines—that is, make the main growing stems or central limbs with a thicker line. When the skeleton limb makes a change of direction, indicate a joint by means of a dot before moving the drawing line off in the new direction. Watch for proportionate lengths of the lines in relation to other lines of the structure and also for the subtleties of the varying angles in changes of linear direction.

FIGS. 1-1 to 1-3

Three plant structure drawings carried out with a broad nib. The result is a clear and bold linear design. The space divisions, linear proportions, and directional movements differ considerably because the natural objects themselves are so different. These three skeletal forms are reasonably regular, but many will be found to be wildly irregular and dynamic.

FIG. 1-1

Weed

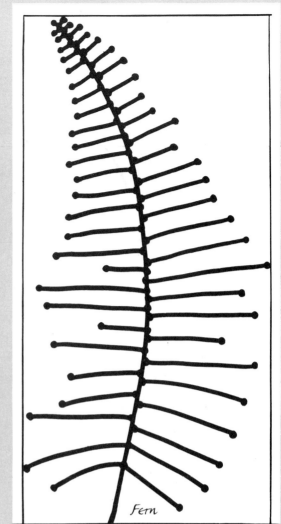

Fern

FIG. 1-2

Weed

FIG. 1-3

When the drawing is complete, enclose it in a black line rectangle and put three or four drawings on one sheet of paper (pad size about 22" x 18") in order to make easy comparisons between them.

CONCLUSIONS

Look at the drawings as they now appear side-by-side. You will notice perhaps for the first time the divsions of space between the limbs of each structure drawing and the relationship in both area size and suggested direction of movement each space-division bears to the other. Such relationships can be studied in the space divisions side-by-side in the same drawing, and then they may be compared with the very different divisions of space occurring in the other structure drawings. Having made this observation, we can now begin to appreciate "flat" [1] space-division design and to be critically aware of how such structure drawings divide up space in so many different ways over an apparently flat two-dimensional surface.

Look again at your sheet of drawings. Which of the structures appears to provide the most interesting visual arrangement of jointed lines and areas of space? You will probably find that the structure having the least symmetrical and least regular space divisions and the fewest parallel lines has the most appeal. This is the first crucial point: Sameness or regularity tends to produce an inanimate and mechanical structure. On the other hand, a linear structure composed of diverse and opposing elements is vital and visually stimulating if held together by a structural unity. (A sense of structural unity is imparted when the organic movement from limb to limb is a characteristic of the structure rather than a contrived, artificial arrangement of the parts.)

The second vital point is that the fundamental form of a skeletal object is not realized by merely following the apparent edges of the object, either when regarding it or when drawing it. The important elements are the proportion of its parts, the joints and directional arrangement of the limbs that are its structural parts, and the nature of the space in and around the object.

---

[1] The word "flat" is used here with some reservations. Space 1 indicates the relationship between two- and three-dimensional space.

12

FIG. 1-4

Byssus threads anchoring young scallops. In this complex linear structure, the space divisions defined by the threads play an important part in our perception of the skeletal form itself. (Shell International Petroleum Company Ltd.)

FIG. 1-5

Decomposed leaf revealing the delicate skeletal structure supporting the "flesh" of the leaf.

FIG. 1-4

FIG. 1-5

We can now summarize the essential characteristics of a skeletal object.

1. Its outward shape is entirely dependent on the articulated structure of its limbs, and the form of the object is *its shape determined by its structure*—hence the importance of understanding structure. For example, we cannot make a valid drawing of the human hand unless we understand the jointed skeleton of the bones that are its underlying structure. The apparent edges of the fingers merely indicate the flesh or clothing of the basic structure.

2. A skeletal object, unlike an object of mass, constitutes a number of parts jointed together as a series of limbs.

3. The linear structure of the object defines the space which the object occupies. A skeletal object breaks up the space around it very considerably through the extension of its limbs. Consequently, we must be aware of the space immediately surrounding and penetrating such an object in order to comprehend its form.

4. An object with a skeletal structure can be represented by a number of lines moving in different directions, but all connected to a main stem by a series of joints in what is known as an "articulated system." Such a drawing will effectively realize the structural form of the object.

Opposed to the skeletal object is a second family of objects composed of mass. A boulder, a pebble, a loaf of bread, and a cloud do not possess limbs. They are objects of volume or mass and will be discussed in Form II (Chapter 4).

Finally, it should be stressed that a close analysis of objects from nature should enable you to solve many different types of design problems calling for either objects having mass or a predominant skeleton. We have been working here with relatively small-scale items, but the structural principles remain the same even with objects of gigantic size.

A famous master at depicting structure was the great French painter, Paul Cézanne, who attempted to render the permanent character of things (see Chapter 12). He spoke of art being "theory developed and applied in contact with nature . . ." of treating nature "by the cylinder, the sphere, the cone, everything in proper perspective so that each side of an object is

FIG. 1-6

ANATOMICAL EXPOSITION
OF A TIGER
George Stubbs
A drawing illustrating the artist's preoccupation with structure. The discernible skeletal form of the rib-cage defines the space-volume of the body, while the bone structure of the limbs, articulating the animal's movements, can also be seen and "felt" just beneath the surface.
(Victoria and Albert Museum, London)

FIG. 1-7

RITE OF PASSAGE

FIG. 1-6

FIG. 1-7

directed towards a central point." [2] But Cézanne did not simply impose an arbitrary geometric formation onto nature; rather, he attempted to reveal structural truths by removing confusion and clutter from visual sensations. He sought to achieve this by deliberately organizing objects within the cone of vision (the natural cone of focus made by the eye when concentrating on any single distant point). Through such an organization Cézanne intended to create an order out of confused visual impressions, for in the natural cone of vision the distant point is in focus, while the rest of the cone produces a periphery of vagueness and confusion. This is what Cézanne meant by "réaliser"; to bring all into ordered focus and thus introduce the artist's structural order into visual sensations.

We repeat one of our initial aims: to heighten the ability to perceive nature through this search for structure (Fig. 1-6). It is important to realize that we have made these skeletal structure drawings from actual objects, that the information has come from outside one's self. Too often the layman imagines that the artist and designer are suddenly struck by a flash of inspiration from nowhere. Usually, however, it is a sharpened faculty of observation and an acute perception that triggers the imaginative vision. A twig structure can suggest a tubular steel chair frame, or the movement of a figure in action (Fig. 1-7). Look at some of the skeletal structure drawings upside down, and see how they change their character completely, suggest new objects and usages. If you will examine the twenty small drawings of tree formations in Fig. 3-4, made by a student walking through the woods, you will notice the many differing space arrangements produced by a relatively few vertical lines, which could be exploited for design purposes. All were derived from observation. A capacity to observe is a necessary part of the beginning student's artistic equipment; and to record what he sees, his sketchbook should always be within handy reach. Finally, note the architectural form of the Brussels Atomium, derived from the skeletal molecular structure of an iron molecule (Fig. 1-8).

---

[2] Sir Herbert Read, *A Concise History of Modern Painting* (London: Thames & Hudson, 1959), p. 17.

FIG. 1-8

THE ATOMIUM, BRUSSELS INTERNATIONAL EXHIBITION (1958)
A. & J. Polak, architects
An example of skeletal structure in architecture. This structure is a model of an iron molecule enlarged 165 million times. It is 360 ft. high.
(The Architectural Review, London)

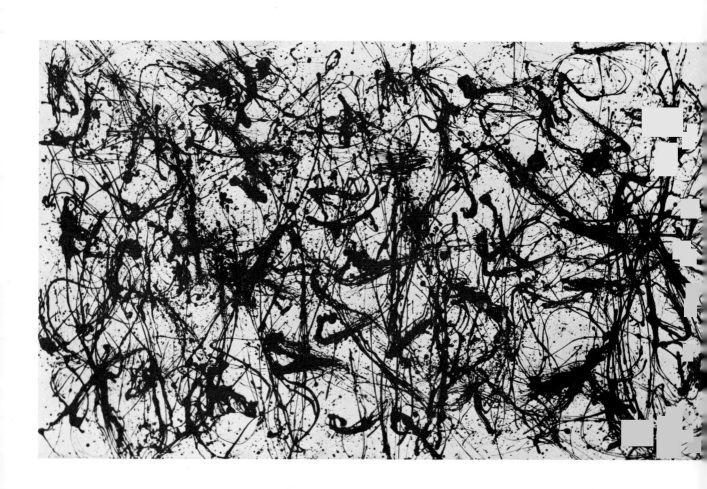

2

lines
and marks
with ink

So much could be written about line quality that it is presumptuous to discuss it in only one chapter of this book. But since this whole book deals with drawing in one form or another, and constant references will be made to "the line," we must at least present a brief introduction to the subject.

When someone draws a line, it is as personal to him as his own fingerprint. Consider the factors involved: a line is a person's direct response, through drawing, to an experience. It may or may not be a sensitive drawing response, for the degree of sensitivity depends on the expressiveness of the person's touch, the quality of his mood, and the type of medium he employs. The use made of lines in Form I was almost mechanical. They were drawn to give certain information in a diagram drawing, and they varied only in weight to distinguish the more important structure lines from the less important. But when a drawing is rendered freely and naturally—more spontaneously—a line governed by "touch," "mood" and "medium" becomes a personal commitment (Figs. 2-1 to 2-4). Your personal response to stimuli will be different from that of your neighbor—therefore your mood, your feeling, will be different, also; and this in turn, will affect your touch sense so that your line or mark will have a unique quality. If you are using charcoal, the results will be quite different from those produced by

19

the medium of pen and ink. If you sing to yourself while draw-ing the line, the line will reflect your mood; if you mutter angrily beneath your breath, then the line, even though de-scribing the same object, will be a different kind of line. Some people are almost hypnotically relaxed in drawing; others feverishly bite their tongue. And as you draw, the paper, de-pending on the type of surface, will set up a resistance to the pen or brush or finger or piece of wood. How you overcome this resistance will obviously also determine the quality of your line. Just contrast for a moment the sensations you would ex-perience in using soft charcoal over a coarse paper surface or using a hard, spiky nib over velvet smooth paper. You can *feel* the kind of line that will result, without having to draw it. The line of drawing, however it is accomplished, evolves from the attempt to reconcile the tensions that exist between perceiving the object and imaginatively re-creating it through drawing— between the factual, substantial reality of the object and the artist's imaginative exploration of it. You may create a line without actually drawing it, where two areas of different tone or color meet in a design.

Throughout this book you will find that drawing is used as the catalyst between knowledge and invention. To draw a thing is to *know* a thing; and from the illustrations, you will see that more value is placed on the direct, personal mark that is the spontaneous result of a person's excitability about an object and the ideas it engenders, or an experience, than on a "neat," technically good, but dead-as-mutton representational drawing.

THE EXPERIMENTS

Starting with a blank sheet of white paper (about 15″ x 22″— rough or smooth, according to preference), try to produce as many different vertical lines as possible, working over the sheet from left to right. First, however, assemble as much drawing "equipment" as possible, from the conventional pen and brush to more unorthodox materials such as rubberbands, pieces of twig or wood, edges of paper, the edge of a thumbnail, hair grips and curlers, and so on—as varied a range of things as can be dipped in black ink to make a line of drawing.

FIG. 2-1

Sheet of experimental lines and marks.

Start at the left with the lightest possible lines (hair lines). Gradually build up as you move across the paper to heavy, thick lines. After this, combine both thick and thin into one line, a swelling line that is alternately thick and thin throughout its whole length. Try doing this first with the pen and the brush and leave a little space between the marks; then, in these spaces, repeat the variations of line, but this time use all the equipment you have gathered together. Experiment with every single piece—metal, wood, bone, paper, or plastic. As the lines go down, be aware of the quality of mark produced—sharp or dull, gray or black, firm or broken—and try to remember the particular "feel" of the instrument that made the mark as it was moving over the paper surface. You will probably remember some that particularly suited you, producing a definite feeling of control and of satisfaction while the line was being made. Finally, draw lines with your left hand, lines starting at the bottom of the paper and finishing at the top, lines where you press hard on your drawing instrument, overcoming strong paper resistance, lines when the instrument is almost dry of ink, and lines when it is flooded with ink. Then, on top of all this, try a few lines which will have a completely different character, lines which you will *print* rather than draw. For example, ink the edge of a ruler, press the ruler onto the paper, and see what you have; repeat this ruler-line, but this time dampen the paper area beneath the ruler and then compare this line with the first. You might even print a line from a piece of string. All these variations—and there are many more you can invent—produce a different line quality.

When this sheet of line marks is complete (Fig. 2-1), it should reveal a wide range of drawing possibilities. To complete these line experiments and to see what kind of free approach to drawing they might have induced, here is a concluding piece of work.

Concluding experiment

Take one of the natural objects used for the structure drawings of Form I (Chapter 1) and redraw it. But this time draw it spontaneously and naturally. Use any drawing instrument and line method (or combinations of them) which you found particularly attractive when making the line sheet. On this occasion, you are not analyzing or probing structure; you have to

FIG. 2-2

Rapidly executed drawings of twigs, using line, blob, and smeared tone.

22

FIG. 2-2

attack the object and work spontaneously and rapidly to complete it in two or three minutes at the most. The drawing you produce will be an *impression* of the object—yet it will be more than this. Your attack is based on knowledge—the knowledge of the fragmentation of space and the line direction determined by the organic quality of the object, which you have learned from previously drawing its skeletal structure. And because your recently gained knowledge of ink marks and lines will help you to "let go" in your quick, two-minute attack, the resulting drawing will be both a swift statement of appearances and a remembered statement of fact. In Figs. 2-2 and 2-3, notice the vitality and immediacy of impact these quick sketches produce, which tell more about the living aspect of nature than any number of careful and labored detailed drawings could do. Drawing of this free and experimental character is constantly demanded throughout the book, and you will find that the sheet of line experiments can be used for constant reference.

FIG. 2-3

A series of rapid twig notes of expressive line quality. A searching for structure can be seen, but no amount of "finished" drawing would capture the sheer feeling for twig form that these spontaneous drawings evoke.

FIG. 2-4

NUMBER 32

FIG. 2-3

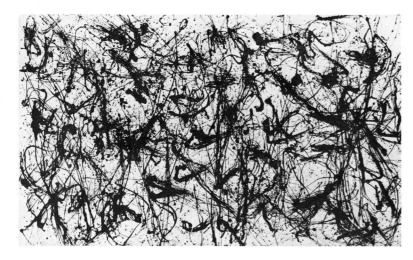

FIG. 2-4

3

the relationship
between
two and three dimensions

The work described in this chapter provides a logical continuation of Form I (Chapter 1), where we made drawings or diagrams that were meant to provide positive information. By means of lines moving out from joints in lateral (that is, two-dimensional) directions we revealed the structural characteristics of an object; and once a frame was placed around this structure drawing, a flat grid pattern emerged. On looking at these finished drawings, the eye is first aware of the areas of space between the lines of the structure and sees them in terms of length and breadth only, or simply as a flat pattern of divisions. Then, gradually, certain other factors become apparent, and we realize that our eyes are apprehending not only up, down, and across, but also in. We find ourselves visually probing the possibilities of the third dimension, depth.

This ability to comprehend depth is a mental-optical faculty we use constantly. Every time you put out your hand to grasp a door handle you make an automatic appraisal of the distance your hand should travel in order to make contact with the handle. Sometimes when this combined optical, mental, and kinesthetic apprehension of space is upset, you will find yourself misjudging the distance and either hitting the door hard with your hand or stopping short in mid-air before reaching the handle. If you close one eye and then reach out to pick up

27

a book, you will find it surprisingly difficult to judge the depth of space involved. Some people are afflicted with a more limited depth perception than others, and such misjudgment of depth can be a frequent cause of highway accidents; a driver making a left-hand turn in front of oncoming traffic may have a collision because he considered the approaching cars far enough way to allow plenty of time for the turn.

We obviously live our lives "in depth." That is, we move and we constantly exist in space. As we found in Form I (Chapter 1), when we isolate any skeletal object in order to look at it more closely, we discover that the space immediately around the object is just as important as is the solid fact of the object itself. Faced with many objects in close juxtaposition, we make a subconscious pinpointing of their positions in space. If we were then blindfolded we would attempt to weave a way among them as we plot their positions on our mental object-in-space screen. This natural ability to see and comprehend a three-dimensional world remains with us and operates even when we are confronted by a flat, two-dimensional surface such as a piece of drawing paper. So long as the paper remains unmarked, no suggestion of space penetration occurs; but put on some lines which start a demarcation of flat areas, and the eye begins to search for depth.

It would be a good thing at this stage to turn back to Form I and look again at the structure drawings. Do any of the spaces between the lines of the structure seem to recede more into the distance than other spaces in the same drawing? Or do some spaces appear nearer than others? Does your eye return to one space which suggests a dominant frontal area? Or does it search out a hole, a receding area? Such a dominant place would be a focal point in the drawing, and it is interesting to note that a focal point can be either a hole or a forward-projecting area. If you notice such a dominant frontal or receding area, then without having recourse to perspective you have produced depth on a flat piece of paper.

Since its inception during the early Renaissance, the method of creating the illusion of depth over a flat surface has been performed by establishing vanishing points and disappearing lines. This perspective has been the traditional means of taking the onlooker into the picture. But this mechanical illusion, by becoming merely a formula, can blind the artist to an inten-

FIG. 3-1

RELIEF CONSTRUCTION IN WHITE, BLACK, AND MAROON
Victor Pasmore
Varying degrees of depth are achieved over this flat surface. Assess for yourself the differing degrees of projection and recession achieved by these lines and rectangular panels. Tonal dominance and line weight and quality produce the spatial perceptions experienced.
(Victor Pasmore)

FIG. 3-2

NORHAM CASTLE
J. M. W. Turner
Turner's landscape dissolves into misty regions of space. Depth is achieved through varying intensities and weights of tone and by the strength of dominant marks. Compare this with the painting of the persimmons by Mu-Ch'i.
(Trustees of the Tate Gallery, London)

FIG. 3-1

FIG. 3-2

sive personal experience of space, to the natural experience of depth perception. And as we have tried to show, natural depth perception does occur without perspective (see Fig. 3-1). The purpose of the following experiment is to create an awareness of *natural* depth perception as opposed to mechanical systems of perspective.

But before going on, it would be well to point out that when the illusion of perspective is used creatively rather than automatically, the result can impart a genuine and personal experience of space. A great authority on Italian Renaissance art, the late Bernard Berenson had this to say about the work of Perugino (1445-1523), the Umbrian (central Italian) painter who was a master of perspective.

> Space composition can take us away from ourselves and give us, whilst we are under its spell, the feeling of being identified with the Universe, perhaps even of being the soul in the Universe. . . . For those of us who are neither idolators nor suppliants, this sense of identification with the Universe is of the very essence of religious emotion—an emotion by the way, as independent of belief and conduct as love itself. . . . The religious emotion, for some of us entirely, for others at least in part, is produced by a feeling of identification with the Universe; this feeling in its turn can be created by space composition. It follows then that this art can directly communicate religious emotion—or at least the religious emotion that many of us really have, good church members though we may be.[1]

Berenson has put his finger on one of the fundamental purposes of art: to heighten man's instinctive awareness of the cosmos and to enable him to identify himself with the vast range of things within the universe. When this new world is revealed by a design, as in the case of Perugino, our instinctive links with the great systems of space, matter, and energy are more consciously realized, and we are "taken away from ourselves." Look at Turner's space in Fig. 3-2. Painters, sculptors, and architects, even though working in abstract forms, today concern themselves with space and our feeling for it; space is one of the permanent conditions of life—and thus of art, as well. Perhaps when man knows more about the space which surrounds him and its relationship with time, the artist will have to change his approach to space and his sensitivity to it may be modified. But at the moment it still remains a vital constituent of our aesthetic response to human experience.

---

[1] Bernard Berenson, *The Italian Painters of the Renaissance* (London: Phaidon, 1952), p. 122.

FIG. 3-3

PERSIMMONS

FIG. 3-4

Twenty notes, made out-of-doors, indicate the wide range of vertical-line space divisions that can be extracted from tree groupings. There are the curvilinear and the straight, the symmetrical and the asymmetrical, the interesting and the dull. They draw one's attention primarily to two-dimensional space in vertical and lateral directions.

FIG. 3-3

FIG. 3-4

THE EXPERIMENTS

The stimulus for the drawings made in Form I came from observing actual skeletal objects; and for the work at hand, we shall also turn to objects in nature. We are to illustrate *space in depth* without having recourse to the more mechanical disappearing lines of perspective—to see, in fact, how a natural depth perception operates. This can best be done by observing rather than by inventing some gimmicky manipulation of abstract geometry. Fifteen minutes outside with a sketch pad and a soft, black drawing crayon will be sufficient. Since we have had some experience now of linear or skeletal structures, we shall retain this kind of form. Look at a clump of tree trunks and note how they are grouped together in bunches of three, four, or five trunks. As you look around, notice the different grouping arrangements of other clumps of trees. On your pad, draw about a dozen small squares, freehand, about 2″ x 2″. In each square, make a simple and direct line sketch of vertical trunks, a different formation in each square for the different clumps you see. These are not meant to be pictorial views of trees; the lines, heavy or light as appropriate, indicating the position of each tree, will serve as notes or diagrams, as in Fig. 3-4. As you make these drawings, you will notice the distance between trees. You will notice the space *sideways* between each tree and also the fact that some of these vertical trunks are *farther back* than others—that there is space between them in depth as well as horizontally.

As you make your drawings, you will probably automatically attempt to show the space in depth by thickening the lines which represent the trees in front, and by so doing you will push the thinner lines to the rear, *together with the space between these thinner lines* (Fig. 3-5). This will produce some depth in the drawing. The horizontal space organization is extremely simple to depict. So now the eye penetrates the drawing to the thinner lines which appear to be behind, as well as crossing the lateral distances between the trunks. One other thing you may have done automatically to increase the apparent depth between the tree lines: you may have started some of the lines higher in the square than others, from the base

FIG. 3-5

Specific frontal areas have now been created by the thickening of certain lines in these three drawings. The greater depth or recession in the bottom drawing is due to the introduction of more delicate, secondary lines.

FIG. 3-6

Unlike Fig. 3-5, this drawing has no differing weight of line to produce frontal or receding regions. Instead, depth is achieved by contrasting the totally enclosed areas (which appear frontal) with the more open regions (which appear to recede) where space can move in and out.

FIG. 3-7

Two drawings where depth perception operates in several ways. Line weight brings forward both line and immediate space. Although no areas are totally enclosed, more open space around a line tends to produce a greater suggestion of distance within this particular rectangular frame. There is also a suggestion of perspective in the size and position of the lines, introduced quite unconsciously by the student; yet it is a lively perspective, not mechanical or dead.

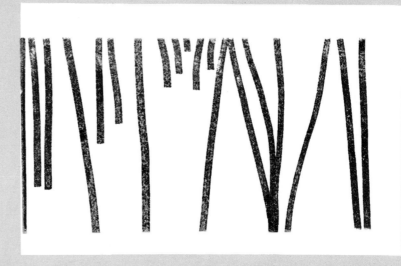

FIG. 3-6

FIG. 3-5

FIG. 3-7

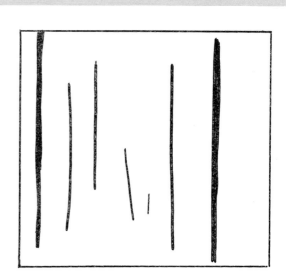

line up to perhaps a third or half the distance up the square (Figs. 3-6 and 3-7).

Conclusions

What significant conclusions are to be drawn from such instinctively produced notations of tree groupings? The three most important ones which are well illustrated in Figs. 3-5 to 3-12 are

1. When an area is not completely contained by lines—when space penetrates it from neighboring areas—the area recedes.

2. The heavier the weight of line, the more frontal dominance it and the surrounding space will have.

3. The quality of a line may also relate to depth. Examine the sheet of lines previously made in Chapter 2 (Fig. 2-1). Sharp, incisive lines come forward; broken, blurred, or gray lines recede. You will notice that even a heavy line that is grayish and "spongy" will appear to be farther back than a much slighter line possessing sharpness and a biting edge quality.

These three points are borne out when they are applied to industrial design artifacts. Look at the refrigerator illustrated in Fig. 3-8. In any visual context, depth perception tends to operate in similar ways.

These three conclusions help explain how your eye, in the first structure drawings in Form I distinguished between frontal areas and receding areas and eventually seized on one area as the dominant focal area. That the eye, or rather that the total visual organization of eye and brain, naturally seeks to measure in depth has already been demonstrated. This analysis of the simple drawings of trees illustrates how the three-dimensional illusion operates in drawing without recourse to the mechanical help of perspective. Since we possess the capacity to be aware of the depth of space occupied by an object, this awareness is obviously an important factor in any visual design. As we said in Form I, an awareness and an appreciation of the space immediately surrounding the object is very necessary to apprehend completely the object itself. The space in's and out's of a piece of furniture (between the legs, through the chair arms) contribute very substantially to our perception of

FIG. 3-8

REFRIGERATOR BY PRESTCOLD
The dominant black strips at top and bottom of the front panel give a strong emphasis to the white region which we thus perceive as a positive region of defined space, rather than form. The stereoscopic sharpness of the handle projects further forward, strongly indicating its function. Our total perception of the form is cunningly aided by these simple devices. (Photograph by Council of Industrial Design, London)

FIG. 3-9

OFFICES FOR BRITISH OLIVETTI
LTD., LONDON
Misha Black and John Diamond, designers
A further example of spatial illusions created through an exploitation of line weight and quality and degrees of tone. Full practical use is made of the wall for the typewriter tables, yet the visual barrier of the wall surface is diminished by exploiting our natural depth perception. The sharp, black frame of the table projects forward from the wall, while the heavy, black "O" on the wall is more frontally dominant than the mosaic trade mark. Thus three regions of depth are suggested, and the wall may be used without being visually or psychologically oppressive. (The Architectural Review, London)

FIG. 3-8

FIG. 3-9

the form of the object, a fact that every designer must take into account. In this chapter we have now developed the space concept somewhat further. Rather than regarding a single form in its individual envelope of space, we have moved into a large space field containing several forms and studied their positions in depth, both in relation to the total space and to each other.

We can now say that form is complementary to space, and space is complementary to form. In painting a landscape or a portrait, in forming a piece of sculpture, or in designing an automobile interior or an office (see Fig. 3-9), this relationship must be taken into consideration.

Concluding experiment

To reinforce this elementary lesson in depth perception, we will present a more developed and more consciously organized problem. Take one of the simple tree trunk studies, and in the studio make a larger and more finished drawing in pen and ink, along the following lines. (About 8″ x 8″ is a good size for this new square, which should be enclosed with a good firm pen line.) Redraw any one of the small sketches in the larger square, with thin, delicate pen lines all of equal weight. This now gives you a design of vertical lines, the special arrangement of which has been taken from an observed source in nature, and in which you have some totally enclosed areas (frontal areas) and some space-penetrated areas (receding areas). But since the lines are all of equal weight, the drawing will not appear very three-dimensional. Now, with a pen or brush, thicken up two lines which almost, or totally, enclose an area, in order to achieve a stronger frontal dominance for that area and for those particular lines. Look over the design again (remember you are no longer thinking about tree trunks) and decide which verticals should be thickened only slightly in order to produce some frontal dominance but not as much as in the first area. In other words, this area will appear behind the first. After these two operations, the design is now composed of three differing weights of line—the forward-thrusting heavy lines, the medium lines in the middle distance, and the thin lines of the original drawing which now appear well recessed. One more thing remains to be done. From the page of line experiments made in Chapter 2, choose one type of line of some definite quality, either very sharp or very diffuse, and

FIG. 3-10

Enlargement from small, outdoor, tree-grouping note. Frontal, middle, and distant regions have been produced with line weight, line quality, and enclosed and open areas. Notice the importance of line quality in such a space context. The thin, yet sharp line in the center of the drawing is almost stereoscopic in its jump forward, despite its lack of weight and its position, surrounded by much empty space.

FIG. 3-11

Subtle depth relationships have been established in this drawing using the four verticals of differing weight and positioning them to allow varying degrees of space penetration within the rectangle. The frontal projecting horizontal bar gives a space-focus to the four verticals and helps the eye to make a more positive assessment of their depth position in space.

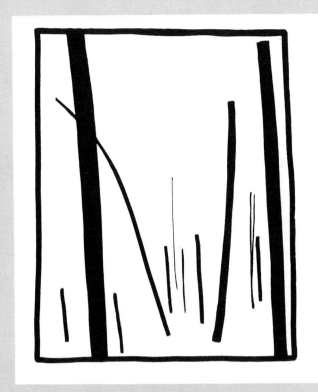

FIG. 3-10

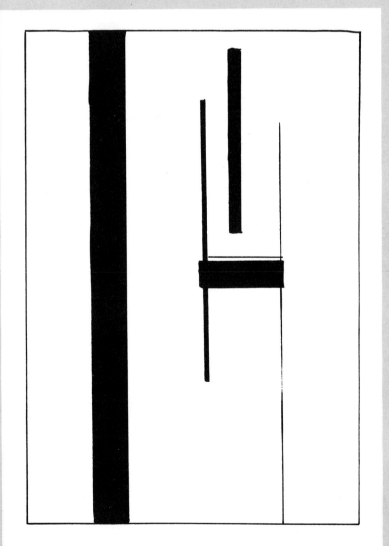

FIG. 3-11

insert a similar line anywhere in this design. Does this line of definite quality appear near or far away in relation to the other black lines? Figures 3-10, 3-11, and 3-12 illustrate similar situations.

The drawing is now complete. Once again, rather like the structure drawings, it has become almost a diagrammatic design, but nevertheless a design giving considerable information. Regions of varying depth have been created, and the vertical lines have a relationship to each other based on their depth positioning rather than on rhythmic, proportional, or tensional considerations.[2] A re-examination of the three "Conclusions" arrived at from our notations on tree groupings should help to clarify why this is so.

SOME FURTHER OBSERVATIONS

While discussing space in depth, it is interesting, and I think necessary, to draw attention to some approaches to art, that achieve a three-dimensional realization of the world through apparently flat, two-dimensional design.

I am referring, of course, to Eastern art and to the art of children the world over. Japanese woodcuts, Chinese scroll paintings, Mogul and Rajput paintings in India, and a six-year-old's drawing from anywhere—all have several factors in common. During the last sixty years, art in the West has finally broken away from the limitations of "realism," from the 600-year-old struggle to portray "appearances" (as depicted by the mechanical rules of perspective) and has utilized some of the flat-pattern techniques of the East and of primitive painters, with no great loss of spatial depth and a definite gain in meaningful expression. Obviously, then, the two-dimensional space of the paper surface can become three-dimensional regions of depth, without the artificial imposition of Western perspective formulas. Our aim in Space I has been to indicate how this can be done consistent with the way we naturally perceive spatial relationships in depth. The "Conclusions" to the first space experiment of this chapter present three specific situations which produce three-dimensional space.

FIG. 3-12

Two drawings which illustrate how varying regions of depth are more obviously perceived when the natural scene is reduced to the linear abstraction. When the natural scene is re-created from the abstraction, as in the drawing on the right, it also gains in depth contrasts over a first, quick sketch.

---

[2] Linear tensions are discussed in Space IV (Chapter 11).

Eastern art (and incidentally some early Western medieval art) uses the size-proportion-color method of achieving emphasis and dominance for the important parts of the design. These are the parts that are ideologically significant, rather than the parts that are visually significant. Most Western artists have found visual significance their greatest concern. In primitive art, for example, the important figure in a composition is drawn as the largest figure, irrespective of his position visually in the design. Conversely, "crowd" figures and unimportant figures are drawn smaller, even if they are in the very front of the picture (Fig. 3-13). Young children do exactly the same thing. They play up the objects and the people in the picture that are important to them, rather than being concerned with visual accuracy. Color is used, too, for producing emphasis and to enrich the decorative effects of the painting rather than to indicate spatial relationships.

The space elements created in this so-called "two-dimensional" art possess depth as a result of frontal dominance achieved by parts of the design, in much the same way as the heavy lines of the tree diagrams were forward-thrusting. This depth is not obvious to Western eyes, so accustomed to the converging lines and diminution of perspective—it is more natural, more subtle (because it has an abstract quality to it), and perhaps more expressive, since the artist is freer to use the space relationships for purely aesthetic ends throughout his work. Perspective can be a very demanding master, and the danger is that the "means" become more important than the ends.

In 1908, the French painter Henri Matisse wrote:

Expression to my way of thinking does not consist of the passion mirrored upon a human face or betrayed by a violent gesture. The whole arrangement of my picture is expressive. The place occupied by the figures or objects, *the empty spaces around them*, the proportions, everything plays a part.

There is little conscious use of perspective in the paintings of Matisse (Fig. 3-14), but depth is created naturally through the organization of his design in the manner we have discussed. The idea that space, empty space, can be expressive was quite a perceptive statement to make in 1908, even though the Japanese print had then been in vogue for some time.

FIG. 3-13

HUNTERS SHOOTING DEER
Fragment of fresco from Alpera, Spain. The deer are the largest objects, irrespective of their space position in the design, because they are the most important objects. (The American Museum of Natural History)

FIG. 3-14

THE JOY OF LIFE
Henri Matisse
Space and form in a complementary association. An example of the expressiveness of Matisse's "empty spaces. . . ." (© 1963 by the Barnes Foundation, Merion, Pennsylvania)

FIG. 3-13

FIG. 3-14

4

structural families:
objects of mass
and the structure of volume

The second family of objects which now concerns us differs in every way from the skeletal forms in Form I. Experience there showed us that when we can determine structure, we must do so if we are to draw with complete understanding; and we also learned that since space often intrudes between the parts of the skeleton, we must take account of the space surrounding such an object if we are to draw successfully its significant proportions, movement, and structure.

Drawing is an act of discovery. Either as a conscious reaction to an objective stimulus or as an act of spontaneous creativity, it is concerned with knowing, and awareness of skeletal structure is one aspect of knowing about form. However, objects that are composed of mass—a pebble or a loaf of bread—have no such skeleton (see the definition of skeletal structure under the heading, "Conclusions" in Form I) and thus form a second family of object-types which may be called the "mass" group (Fig. 4-1). Such objects are not made up of a jointed series of skeletal parts, are usually static rather than vibrant, and have a "lumpy" or "massive" quality—characteristics in direct contrast to the linear objects we first examined. And it is not easy to look at a pebble and decide how it can be structurally explained in visual terms. Nevertheless, if one sets out to determine how a sense of structure operates with these solid objects,

FIG. 4-1

MUSE
Constantin Brancusi
Bronze on stone base. An object of mass. The highly polished surface of this heavy swelling mass invites your hand to experience its fullness and appraise its weight. It is the very antithesis of the skeletal object.
(Portland Art Museum, Oregon. Photograph by Eliot Elisofen)

43

how their form and weight and space displacement are apprehended through observation, then one does discover a common structure characteristic which is effective in explaining them in drawing. This structural characteristic operates in a way very different from the skeletal limbs of the first group. See Fig. 4-2, which shows the natural contour line in a piece of wood.

Let us call this common structure characteristic for objects of mass the "continuous contour line." It moves without any break over and around the planes and curved surfaces of a solid form object, constantly making a progression in its exploration of surface and surface inclination (Fig. 4-3). This contour line is both imaginary and real. For many people, as their eyes travel over the surface of a form, they trace "lines of information" relevant to the surface under observation rather as if the tips of the fingers were exploring the form. In some cases, the tactile and the visual senses are so intimately attuned that it is possible to "feel" a surface on one's fingertips merely by intensive looking. The contour line, traveling over and around the surface, is apprehended imaginatively even when it disappears from view around the other side of the object. The following illustration is a good example of this interoperation of the senses. If you were asked to estimate the weight of a watermelon placed before you, your eyes would travel over the surface, appraising the swell and form of the surface, to judge the total mass or weight. They would repeat their assessment on the side that is out of sight; and at the same time, you would be imaginatively "feeling" the heaviness of the melon in your hand. The continuous contour line does all this with an object of mass, *entirely through drawing*. It defines solid form as these different levels of perception, sight and touch, work together.

At this stage, a complication occurs, inasmuch as the title of this section refers to "the Structure of Volume," for volume has a dual role. Volume denotes the space occupied by solid form or mass but it also signifies defined regions of space. Volume may refer to a solid like a pebble (Fig. 4-4), or to emptiness like a hole (Fig. 4-5). There is no real contradiction here: there are two kinds of volume that exist independently of each other or can exist side-by-side as properties of the same object. A

44

FIG. 4-2

Photographic magnification of a small wood piece. The contour delineation of the mass is well shown. This photograph could illustrate planes and curved surfaces (Form V) and become an aerial view of a rocky canyon. It is only a question of scale. (Photograph by Wayne Bitterman)

FIG. 4-3

A good, natural example of an object of mass whose form is defined by a continuous contour groove. Notice how the light and shade assists the groove in our perception of the mass.

FIG. 4-4

A hole. This simple, round stone is made the more significant because, through the hole, we become aware of the other side.

FIG. 4-5

Compare this shell with the human ear. It is an object which defines space-volume most delicately.

FIG. 4-6

FROG EATING A LIZARD
Eduardo Paolozzi
Bronze sculpture. On skeletal limbs stands this fearsome form of mass and volume. The holes give suggestions of its mysterious space-cavity, while the projections and protrusions of its surface suggest a molten growth. (Martha Jackson Gallery, New York)

FIG. 4-2

FIG. 4-3

FIG. 4-4

FIG. 4-6

FIG. 4-5

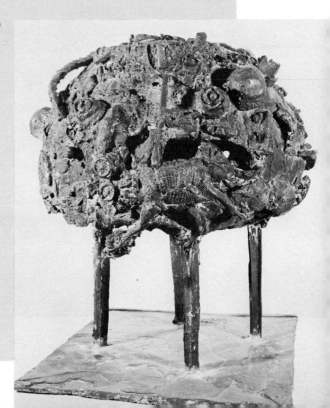

stone is mass volume; an egg or a snail shell is space volume. But volume, to have any discernible shape, must be defined; and this is the important function of the continuous contour line; it will define the space volume of a hole or the mass volume of a rock; and where the rock is pierced with holes, the same contour line will define both kinds of volume (see Fig. 4-6). It will be easier to understand this by looking at the illustrations, Figs. 4-7 to 4-9.

It will be apparent that both Figs. 4-7 and 4-9 are contour drawings which express mass volume—the solidity of the form is reasonably apparent, and the structural shape characteristics of the surface of a mass are defined by the contour line. The figures represent two different kinds of pebbles. By contrast, Fig. 4-8 is a drawing of space volume; the contour line encloses a volume of space rather than a solid form, and it appears as a square hole into which you could place a finger (see also Fig. 4-10). These three illustrations show how effective is the continuous contour line in drawing both volume of mass and volume of space. Try to imagine the pebbles in Figs. 4-7 and 4-9 if they were outlined, only. Would this convey any sense of the structural implication of their surface, or their space displacement or heaviness?

One more factor remains to be introduced into contour-line structure drawing, that of the quality and weight of line. We became acquainted with this important factor in both Drawing Marks I and Space I. It is further illustrated in Figs. 4-11 and 4-12, which indicate how the introduction of line quality and line weight modify one's perception of the form.

You will see that in Fig. 4-12 the heavier weight of the line and the more incisive quality of line are at the "front" of the form, and the line becomes more neutral and less positive as it moves away down the form. In Fig. 4-11, however, these linear emphases are reversed, and our perception of this form is different. By its linear emphases Fig. 4-12 suggests the structure of a hollow space and Fig. 4-11 appears to be a more solid object. A further study of the two illustrations reveals that this difference between "hole" and "solid" is achieved by using linear emphasis in a way that can be stated simply as follows: *If the dominant emphases of weight and quality are introduced where the revolving line converges, an object of more solid*

FIG. 4-7

Contour - line diagrammatic drawings of mass form.

FIG. 4-8

Contour - line diagrammatic drawing of space-volume.

FIG. 4-9

FIG. 4-10

STAIRWAY IN BERLIN
The structure of space-volume revealed in architecture. Here is the continuously revolving contour line defining a hole in a building in the same way that you defined a hole in a piece of wood.
(Ullstein, Berlin. Photograph by Fritz Eschen)

FIG. 4-11

Contour line expressing a projection of form.

FIG. 4-12

Contour line expressing a recession or hole.

FIG. 4-7

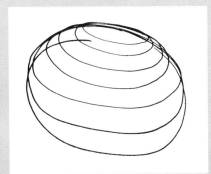

FIG. 4-8

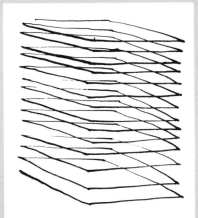

FIG. 4-9

FIG. 4-11

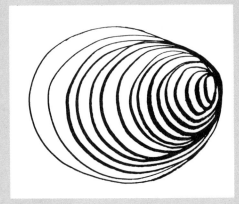

FIG. 4-10

front

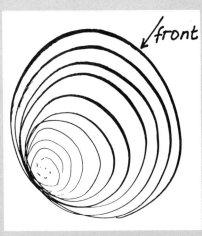

FIG. 4-12

form is perceived. When the reverse is true, and *the revolving contour-line quality is lighter and less sharp in the regions of convergence, then a hollow space form is perceived.* This proposition is consistent with the *frontal dominance* or *recession in space* discoveries made in Space I.

But the contour line, like all things perceived by human sight, suggests different things to different people. Although it gives structural suggestion to volume, it is not always immediately apparent *which* volume: that of space or mass. A longer look at Figs. 4-11 and 4-12 will render you undecided as to which is which. Now the reinforcement to the contour line is to be found in the conventional use of light and shade. The drawings in Fig. 4-13 indicate how, by determining the regions of highlight and shadow and "building them into" the contour structure, a more positive perception of hollow form or solid form can be achieved.

THE EXPERIMENT

Contour lines that are continuously exploring surface or space-volume demand exceptionally free and unforced drawing (Fig. 4-14). The whole arm, rather than just the wrist or the fingers must move, and a rhythm must be built up while the drawing is in progress. The first experiment will help to achieve this rhythmic freedom. Draw on your paper a large freehand shape and "pierce" it with holes of differing shapes and sizes.

Attempt to go deep—and in some cases right through—by using a continuously revolving contour line which varies in its quality and in its weight. Within the same freehand shape try to "pull out" a few projections to contrast with the holes and do not be afraid of any experimentation, such as dropping a blot of ink onto the paper and allowing your revolving line to grow out of the blob. A study of Figs. 4-15 and 4-16 will indicate some idea of the possible inventive variations produced by this exploratory structure drawing. Figure 4-16, particularly, reveals how the surface movement of form, its holes and projections, can be expressed with the rhythmic freedom of the contour line.

FIG. 4-13

A sequence of experiments with the contour line in drawing holes and projections, with conventional tone shading used to supplement the contour line and heighten our perception of the mass or space. Black tone (shadow) helps to suggest how deep is the hole, while highlights catching projecting surfaces help to indicate the degree of projection possessed by the mass. Here, black suggests recession rather than frontal projection because we associate darkness with the depth of a hole. In the context of a projecting form, strong white tone comes forward because we associate the projecting high point of a mass with light reflection. This reverses the natural depth perception discussed in Space I and reveals the difficulty of postulating rules of perception, for—depending on the context—there is an ambiguity about our perception of form and space in which "meaning" plays an important role. This might be termed the factor of psychological association in perception.

FIG. 4-13

Now let us be more objective and examine in detail the human ear. You will notice that its form is made up of a series of holes or hollows situated between projecting ridges. Were you to take a photograph and make a tremendously enlarged print, the ear would look just like an aerial view of a mountain range. It is this very quality of hollows and ridges that the contour line is suited to describe and with which the whole of this chapter has been concerned. But first make a conventional drawing of the ear, in any medium you wish, to produce as accurate a representational drawing as you can with line and tone shading. Second, make a continuous contour-line structure drawing of the same ear, showing all the surface movements, all the holes, and all the projecting ridges. Work very objectively. Use the line as boldly as in making the holes in the freehand shape. By the time you have finished this structure drawing it will probably resemble a contour map of a hilly ground area, rather than a drawing of an ear, such is the definition of surface movement. Yet if we are to make a comparison between the two drawings, the representational and the structural (see Fig. 4-17), I think you will agree that it is the contour drawing that tells you more about the structure of the ear and the organic relationship between the parts of the ear. In making such a structure drawing, it becomes necessary to understand "how" the ear is, in order to re-create it as a form with structural and organic reality.

Conclusions

Objects of mass and the dual nature of volume have now been tentatively explored through structural drawing. If we add skeletal objects to objects of mass and volume, we have examples from each of the two principal families of form. It is very difficult to think of any kind of form which does not take its place in either of these families—from the substantial object, or the shell which is merely a defined region of space, to the hairlike thread.

This emphasis on structure is not just a frill. An attempt was made in Form I to relate structure to the process of comprehending form. Drawing is meaningless without it. Leonardo da Vinci and many lesser artists have attempted to establish that art (and drawing is the foundation of art) is a mental

FIG. 4-14

A typical student sheet of practice drawing with the contour line. The line's insistence on expressing volume, both mass and space, is shown here.

FIG. 4-15

A drawing, made without reference to any object, of a wood form having holes and projections.

FIG. 4-14

FIG. 4-15

activity and a science searching for objective reality. In the present day, we admit that it is also an intuitive, sometimes clairvoyant means of revelation about life, individual consciousness, and subjective experience. The searching for the structural "how" of an object is a mental part of the process of perception when one is looking with intent. Eventually, this search for the structure becomes an intuitive faculty of the artist or designer, for without it drawing can become second to photography. Both your studies of the ear were from direct observation. The traditional drawing is a portrait of a particular ear with emphasis on its sensory appearance in terms of what the eye sees. The contour drawing, while still faithful to local peculiarities, is nevertheless concerned with an "earness" common to all ears everywhere—an absolute quality of earness —and has resulted from what you *know* about the ear, after analysis of its surface mass, as well as what you see. The knowing is as important as the seeing.

In writing this, I realize how misleading these separations can be. The world's great works of art embody a complete marriage between appearance and structure, knowing and seeing, feeling and understanding, all synthesized by the catalyst of vision. Art is art. When one explains art, there is no art. Here lie the difficulties for the writer and the teacher dealing with the visual creative process.

Knowledge of this family of form—of mass or volume objects with which this section has been concerned—has wide application. The cylindrical stalk of a plant, clouds and holes in clouds, eyes situated in sockets, the mass of a boulder, the volume of the human thigh—these are perceptively realized through the structural implications of the revolving contour line. The drawings in Fig. 4-18 are good illustrations of an exploratory search for mass and volume. Would these forms be as graphic without the drawings' insistence on surface contour?

It becomes apparent from structure drawings that by an objective process of reduction to structural realities, we find one way to arrive at the abstract form in art. It was Paul Cézanne, in fact, whose research in this direction charted the path to cubism.[1] From there it was a short step to the abstract or nonrepresentational form; for in delving this deep into structure,

---

[1] See reference to Cézanne in the Conclusion to Form I.

FIG. 4-16

Drawing of an imaginary wood form. Contour line expresses the various surface movements and rhythms.

FIG. 4-17

A first, observed drawing of the human ear and a contour-line structure drawing which heightens perception of the surface movement of the form, of the "plains" and "ridges" of the ear.

FIG. 4-16

FIG. 4-17

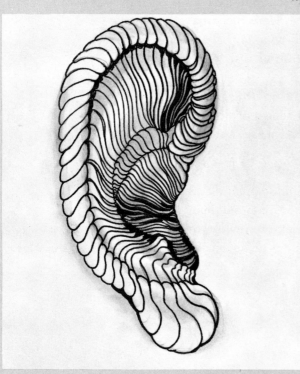
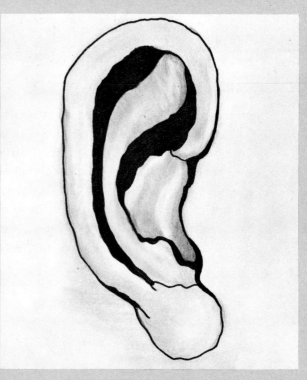

new shapes emerged, derived from the object, yet now existing in their own right. Once the artist realized that such nonrepresentational shapes possessed an aesthetic content and power in their own right, then it was but a short step to produce such abstract forms without recourse to an object at all. And thus nonobjective art was born.

SKELETAL STRUCTURE AND VOLUME

Even the slenderest twig has weight and volume. Although predominantly linear or skeletal in appearance, it is, nevertheless, also an object of mass and volume, as we would see if we were to cut through it and expose a cross section.

The branching marine animal to which the queen scallop is attached (Fig. 4-19) is essentially skeletal, yet its limbs, too, have roundness and volume.

In short, all skeletal objects are also objects of mass and volume. It does not work in reverse, however: objects of mass do not automatically have a skeleton. What, then, is the point of dividing objects into two families if fundamentally they all possess volume? The reason is that we want to bring out the dominant structural characteristic. Everybody would agree that the branching marine animal of Fig. 4-19 is predominantly a linear, multi-directioned, articulated object. This is so obviously its principal structural characteristic that its volume does not intrude greatly on our perception of the object. But look at Fig. 4-20, a brain coral formation from Samoa. Here the situation is the other way around; it is the object's *volume* that we principally perceive, even though it is made up of a series of fine linear branches.

Thus the division of objects into structural families is based on our perception of the dominant structural aspect of the object—whether linear and skeletal or volume and mass. And we are now familiar with the methods of structural drawing which best reveal the skeletal or the voluminous type of form. For example, since we perceive the brain coral predominantly as volume, we should draw it with the continuous contour line, to express its volume, and then put in the skeletal formation to indicate the linear means by which the volume is achieved. In

FIG. 4-18

Contour-line diagrammatic experimental drawings describing volume and mass.

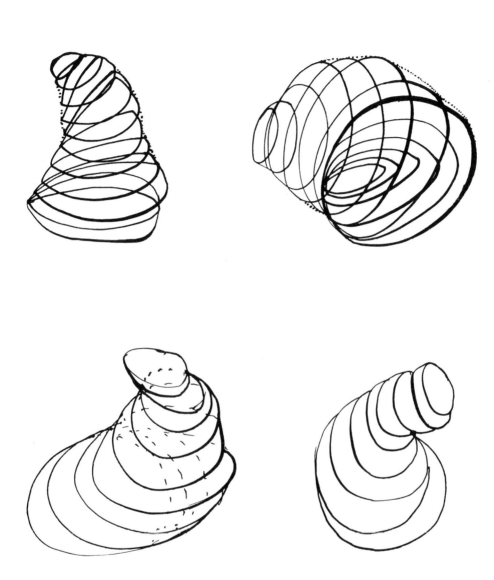

the case of the marine animal, its predominantly linear and branching form is best revealed by drawing it first as a jointed skeletal line. But since a line has no volume, we could add contour lines *around* the skeletal line to give the animal mass.

An imaginative use of both methods of structural drawing can often help reveal the dominant form of an object. A bottle, for example, is pure volume. It is not made up of delicate linear branches like the brain coral, and it has no skeletal form present in its structure. Yet, in drawing the bottle, it helps to draw an imaginary skeletal structure around which the volume can expand. This is suggested in the experiment described in Vision II, where, before drawing the space volume of the bottle, an imaginary skeleton composed of a central vertical line and horizontal "width" lines is drawn. This plots the shape and proportion of the volume which the contour line will then describe. A bottle drawn in this way results from an intelligent application of the principles behind structural drawing, rather than from a mechanical use of a formula.

FIG. 4-19

Branching marine animal with queen scallop. Although our perception of this form is primarily of a skeletal object, the volume or mass aspect of its limbs is also realized in this photograph. (Shell International Petroleum Company Ltd.)

FIG. 4-20

Brain coral from Samoa. Our perception of this form is primarily of an object of mass or volume, yet the coral is made up of many fine skeletal threads.

FIG. 4-19

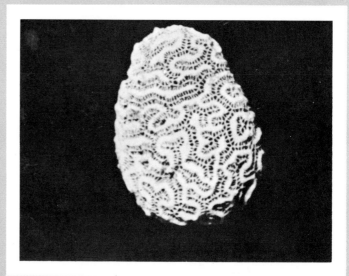

FIG. 4-20

5

the aesthetic implications of form

Examining form in terms of structure, we have come to the conclusion that two basic family types exist: skeletal form and mass form. We discovered structural qualities that are capable of description through drawing and that enlighten our understanding of "how" an object is. They help our eye, mind, and instinct to operate together in appraising the *modus operandi* of the object when it confronts us and demands comprehension rather than mere identification. An awareness of structure directs our attention and interest to search for the inner, more permanent nature of the object. It helps us to recognize associational affinities with other objects and insures that we perceive more about an object than merely the shape of its external appearance. This is the importance of work in structural analysis.

In Form I, we said, "Form or outward shape is dependent entirely on structure. . . ." Although this is true, it would be a mistake at this stage to pursue too far the separation between skeleton and clothing. This section, therefore, will serve as an introduction to the aesthetic implications of form as a complete phenomenon. Webster's definition of form as "the shape and structure of anything" is concise and adequate, but it does not go far enough for the artist who wants to imply that form has an *aesthetic potential*, that the "shape and structure

BIRD IN SPACE (1919)
Constaintin Brancusi
Bronze, 54 inches high.
The soaring of a bird or the
human spirit, symbolized
and suggested through form.
(Collection, The Museum of
Modern Art, New York)

59

of anything" provokes some kind of reaction in the beholder. I would prefer to define form as "a particular organization of shape capable of arousing the emotional and intellectual participation of the individual."

From a potato to an orchid, a jam jar to a Cellini saltcellar, form is inescapable. Even with closed eyes we can appreciate form through our sense of touch. The form of things comprises the total substantial element of our world and is a large part of our conscious orientation. We all have personal reactions of thought and feeling to the ubiquitous presence of form. At the lowest level comes the simple act of accepting or rejecting something when we are shopping. At the highest level comes an experience of recognition, understanding, and sympathy so intense that it approaches ecstasy—a complete self-identification with the object through a heightened total consciousness. It can happen when one is confronted with some extraordinary quality of completeness in the forms of nature, when one is face to face with a work of art, inspiring and transcendental like a Gothic cathedral, a Renaissance bronze figure, a Baroque altarpiece, or even a primitive clay vessel.

There is obviously a distinction to be made between the commonplace and the powerfully moving. When form appears complete and unalterable, when we sense that any addition or subtraction would ruin this completeness, when form is charged with meaning, when it coincides with our desires, invites our physical or imaginative possession and the subsequent loss of our own identity in self-identification with the form—when we are affected in any of these ways, then for a moment we become involved with the mystery of an aesthetic response. For some, this is an intimation of the divine. It is what Bernard Berenson meant in his comments on Perugino's space composition, quoted in Space I—an aesthetic experience of a visual nature. Perugino heightens our awareness of space sufficiently for us to become significantly involved. This kind of experience accounts for an artist's being moved by form and a designer's preoccupation with it. (If we must have a pot to cook in, why not have one to enjoy aesthetically?)

Between the highest and lowest levels of such experience lie many levels of degree. Yet all form contains some interest and audience involvement, for we react to what might be called "pure" form, to squareness or roundness or sharpness (Figs. 5-1, 5-2), irrespective of any meaning the form may have. The sculptor who is actually handling three-dimensional

FIG. 5-1

Two stones from a river bed, shaped by the flow of water. They are magnificent manifestations of "roundness." Herein lies their aesthetic implication.

FIG. 5-2

A river-bed stone that is beautiful in its thin, rounded, flatness. Compare it with the stones of Fig. 5-1. This one arouses different sensations and ideas.

FIG. 5-1

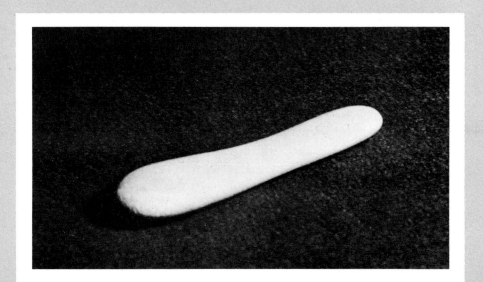

FIG. 5-2

form may be more interested than the painter in these "pure" aspects of form. The sculptor may find motivation in the "pure" form of a potato, whereas the painter would have no interest in it at all. Yet both artists' range of interest in form spreads more widely and more acutely than that of the nonartist.

In nature, "pure" form and meaningful form are to be found side-by-side: the white, smooth bone and the rough, weathered rock; the folds of the hills and the swell of abdomen and breasts in the human torso. It may be the "pure" form that excites the artist, or it may be the significance for him of its meaning—but more than likely both of these aspects of form are inseparably bound up in his aesthetic awareness. For man is still part of the natural world, and forms in nature can stir in him the recognition of common affinities between all forms and their presence in his own physical shape (Fig. 5-3). Such a recognition provides a glimmer of truth—the truth of common qualities of shape among things, and this is a fundamental part of aesthetic awareness (Figs. 5-4 and 5-5).

This chapter touches on only the essential aspects of the aesthetic implications of form. The meaning of beauty and perfection, the psychology of aesthetic sensitivity, the urge for possession, and the faculty to identify with the object—all of which are part of our innate sensitivity to form—must be left to more specialized writing.[1] It is sufficient enough in the early stages of an involvement with art to be aware of the intimate part played by form in stimulating our desires, our moods, our imaginings, our hopes and fears. Knowledge of form is the basis of a whole range of visual imagery which includes both memory of the past and imaginative explorations of the future. What, for example, is "mountain-form"? You have seen mountains, and a generalized image of mountain-shaped characteristics remains with you; you live with the memory-form of the mountain rather than with the mountain. But have you seen an Angel or a Spirit? Probably not. In that case, what form might such an airy creature have? You will be familiar with art's treatment of such things over many hundreds of years—idealized human bodies wearing long flowing garments and often sprouting wings from somewhere around the shoulder blades—a treatment determined by using a form

---

[1] Cf. Kenneth Clark, *Moments of Vision* (Oxford: The Clarendon Press, 1954); Herbert Read, *The Meaning of Art* (Baltimore: Penguin Books, Inc., 1961); Laszlo Moholy-Nagy, *The New Vision and Abstract of an Artist* (New York: George Wittenborn, Inc., 1947).

FIG. 5-3

IDEAS FOR SCULPTURE (1941) Henry Moore sketchbook *Forms of nature, developed into shapes of heightened aesthetic implication by the artist's vision through drawing. (Henry Moore)*

FIG. 5-4

Compare this stone from the river bed with the Cycladic head of Fig. 5-5. This form suggests "head," and it is powerful in the natural state, with just a hint of the features of the face. Its mysterious authority would be lost if the features became intelligible.

FIG. 5-5

CYCLADIC HEAD FROM KEROS *The head simplified to an abstract form by "primitive" artists of the Aegean, about 3000 B.C. The fine simplicity of the form, like the stones taken from the river bed, makes a strong aesthetic appeal per se. Add to this its significance as a symbol of the human head, and we have a powerful object. (Musée du Louvre, Paris. Photograph by M. Chuzeville)*

FIG. 5-3

FIG. 5-4

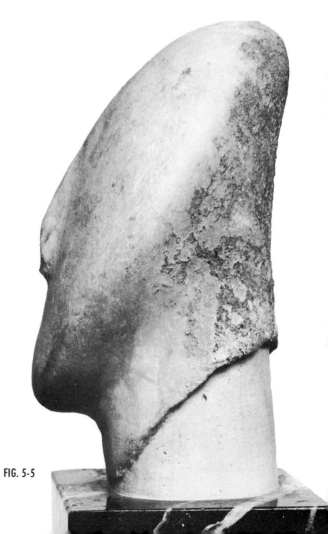

FIG. 5-5

(the human figure) already known to the artist and embellishing it with symbols of purity and flight. Modern art has tackled this problem much more imaginatively, particularly in sculpture, where new and powerful forms have denied any representational allegiance to the human body and have evoked powerful and mystical suggestions of pure "Spirit" (see Fig. 5-6). This is the creative function of art: to produce form in a variety of mediums, form which is capable of enlarging our own individual experience and constantly revealing hidden aspects of life and nature.

The mystery of Francis Bacon's intangible materializing shapes (Fig. 5-7) are a painter's forms to which we react with a feeling of foreboding. In contrast, the distillation of maternal tenderness and madonna-like innocence in Fra Filippo Lippi's "Virgin" (Fig. 5-8), expressed through the translucent and evocatively modeled head and column of the neck, attains a quality of remoteness and spirituality that is almost spine-tingling in its unearthiness. It is the quality of Lippi's form that says all these things to us.

We live surrounded by form: landscape, the human figure, the dream, the legend and the myth, the fantastic minutiae of biochemistry or nuclear physics, the products of industry, commercial advertising, architecture, and townscape, the teeming complexities of nature. We retain images of the shape of all these things. If there is no form, then space is all that remains. (But we shall see in Chapter 12, "Form and Space," that we would not be aware of space without the marker buoys of form to chart it.) This is one of the difficulties in trying to imagine an immortal spirit.

Because of ever-present form and our inescapable involvement with it, architects, designers, and town planners must always consider the aesthetic implications of the objects they sponsor. Living in a visual slum is hardly likely to foster human creative aspirations, and such creativity is a part of the scale on which we measure "progress" and civilization. We live surrounded by too much visual squalor that is made-made—hence our frequent refreshment at the springs of nature, our urge to get into the country "away from it all" (Fig. 5-9).

"The shape and structure of anything," this is the dictionary definition of form, to which we have added an aesthetic qualification. Through our mysterious capacity to be affected by form, we find ourselves in love with all kinds of things. At one and the same time we both belong to the world and yet

FIG. 5-6

BIRD IN SPACE

FIG. 5-7

FRAGMENT OF A CRUCIFIXION
Francis Bacon
A spirit of unease and foreboding haunts these macabre, materializing forms. Here are a painter's forms possessing aesthetic implications not of beauty, but of truth, the truth of the horror of crucifying. (Hanover Gallery, London)

FIG. 5-8

LA MADONNA COL BAMBINO
E ANGELO
Fra Filippo Lippi
The form of the neck and head of this madonna evokes an imaginative response to the theme of maternal, yet virginal, womanhood. (Uffizi Gallery, Florence)

FIG. 5-9

Man-made visual squalor.

FIG. 5-6

FIG. 5-7

FIG. 5-8

FIG. 5-9

transcend it through this aesthetic sensitivity which allows us to possess it so intimately.

As we have stressed several times now, drawing must constantly be used by a student as a means of realizing aspects not immediately discernible in an object. Presenting things in this way, the drawing offers new suggestions of form to be studied, responded to, and then imaginatively developed into a more significant graphic image. Drawing is the principal way the artist brings form into being. At this point it is now possible to make the equation:

FORM = shape derived from structure + aesthetic aura

These factors have been separately discussed; first, the two main structure families of form and the dependence of shape on structure; second, in the implications of the aesthetic aura of form as it occasions a response in the individual. In Drawing Marks I, the expressive and meaningful nature of lines and marks was introduced, and the student was initiated into the possibilities of a personal quality in drawing, by means of a line that is vital, yet sensitive—spontaneous, yet considered. It has been stressed also that objects exist in space and that an awareness of space displacement or space entry plays an important part in an act of perception. It is with all these things in mind—the structure and aesthetic of form, the means of drawing, and the implications of space—that you should approach the following suggested projects.

One factor involved in this work, however, has not yet been touched upon. This is the factor of the imagination, which usually operates at some level when one makes any kind of personal statement, either verbally or visually in drawing. When one is concerned with design—in this case the making of a new form for a specific result—it is the imagination which suggests the development from one stage to another through a series of drawings. But this aspect of the creative process is the sole concern of the experiments in Part Two, "Vision," and we shall not pause to discuss it here. We shall apply our recently gained structural and spatial knowledge to a personal drawing statement.

THE EXPERIMENTS

Use a rough or smooth-surfaced drawing paper (according to taste), minimum size about 16″ x 16″; a pen, brush, or finger, with ink, or a charcoal stick, or pencil. Make a free, and yet

FIG. 5-10

These weathered wood forms, drawn without reference to any object, are dependent upon the contour line to express their mass and their space-volume or holes.

FIG. 5-11

A piece of driftwood drawn with the contour line where the surface direction of the mass demanded emphasis.

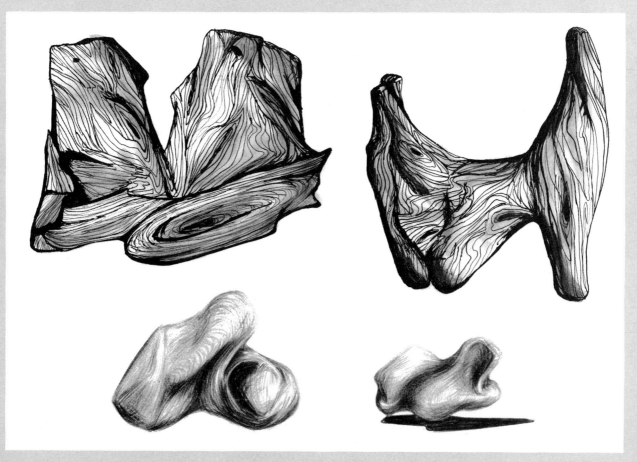

FIG. 5-10

FIG. 5-11

considered, design of the form suggested by each of the following propositions. Start by tentatively exploring the possibilities in drawing loosely, and perhaps vaguely, on a newsprint pad, filling the sheet with suggestions after the manner of doodling. Gradually, your drawing will become more definite as you find one shape suddenly appearing more interesting than the others. Begin to exploit and develop this shape, or a part of it newly discovered, into a fuller indication of the form it suggests. Even when this stage is reached, it is still a good thing to let it continue to evolve through several drawings, before turning to make the finished drawing. Look back for a moment at Henry Moore's drawings for sculpture, to see the progressive shaping of form by drawing (Fig. 5-3).

Use all your resources for this design. Conjure up shapes from memory, build shapes in the mind, "feel" the form as the line explores the paper; allow your knowledge of structure—the jointed limbs of the skeleton or the contour line of the mass—to direct your line. Sense the aesthetic aura emanating from this new thing beginning to grow before you on the paper. Let it grow, rather than try to visualize it before drawing. Start by "scratching about," and fill the wastepaper basket with rejected sheets; but when the drawing is finished, attempt to analyze your aesthetic response to it in terms of the statements made in this text.

Experiment 1

A single and integral free-standing form. Imagine a free-standing rock or wood form which has been weathered by all the elements over a long period of time.

Do you see this as a skeletal object or as a mass/volume object? How does it intrude into space? How does space enter it: through cracks, holes, or tunnels? What is its surface quality as you run your hand over it? Is it the kind of form to be associated with the sound of a high-pitched shriek or with the sound of a dull thud? All these and similar imaginative questions should be running around in your head as the design develops. And do not be afraid to experiment with drawing marks as you feel the need to express special vital elements in the character of your form (see Figs. 5-10 to 5-12).

Experiment 2

A conglomerate form, not free-standing. Consider a bird's-eye view of a section of a dried and rock strewn river bed.

FIG. 5-12

An imaginative metamorphosis of form. The once solid rock has been broken down into what is almost a skeletal object. Compare this imaginative drawing with Fig. 4-20, the brain coral from Samoa.

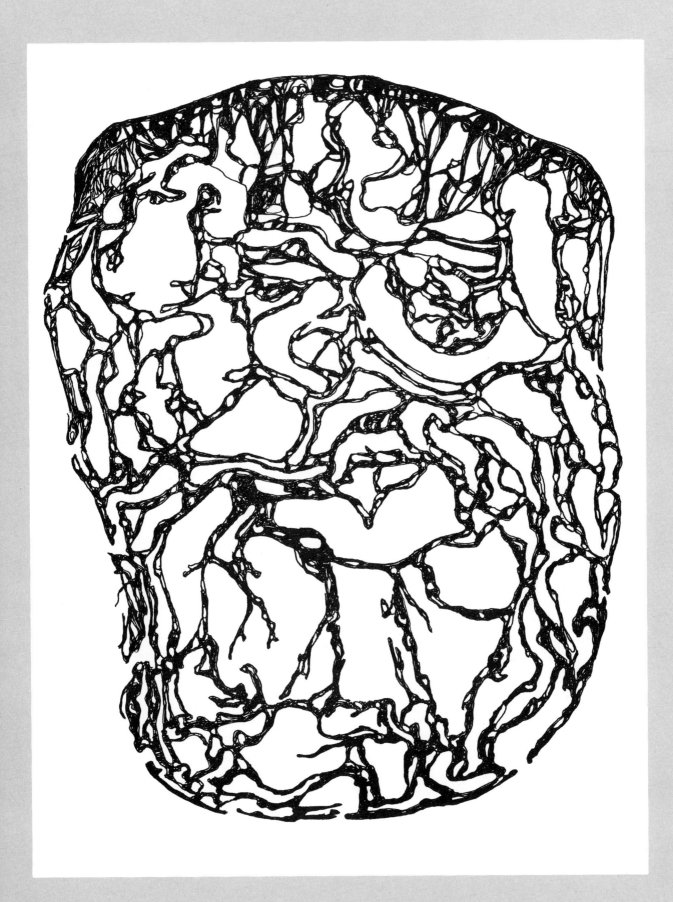

Unlike Experiment 1, which concerns itself with a single monolithic presence, this experiment suggests a more mobile, flowing situation in which many small and independent elements come together to make a compound form. Engagement with this type of form introduces a completely new consideration—the factor of forces, the special study of Space IV, "Dynamic Relationships." Later, when we discuss how forces operate in space to create shifting and fluid organizations of conglomerate form, we shall refer back to this experiment, in which we let our intuition and present knowledge compensate for a lack of knowledge about forces; we depend here on our familiarity with form and space.

Large pebbles, small pebbles, big rocks, all either sharp or smooth, lie on the river bed. But the *way* they lie on the river bed is determined by the water flowing over them, the force involved in this imaginative proposition. The composite form created by the many rocks and pebbles has been created by the force of water. Consequently, the design should show the directional flow of water currents over the stones and account for their clustering and positioning in terms of the water's force. A large stone will act as a barrier to water and to smaller moving pebbles—hence a cluster is formed around a larger or more powerful unit. This is often a characteristic of conglomerate form. Thus two things are happening here: water is flowing smoothly and then a barrier is created which will cause a new direction of water flow. With a new direction of flow, new forces are exerted on the arrangement of other pebbles. These pebbles will, in turn, set up their own opposition and barriers. It is a constantly changing pattern. But, again, such impermanence is a characteristic of conglomerate form.

In the summer when there is no water, the rocks and pebbles exist as a witness to the force that created their formal arrangement. The drawing, when complete, should indicate all these things. The form will have no real beginning and no obvious ending, for it is constantly attracting and expelling the units which shape it. One aesthetic element of this created form will lie in the degree of credibility achieved by the drawing through recognition of how the form was achieved (see Figs. 5-13 and 5-14).

FIG. 5-13

In this river-bed drawing, form is less important than force and movement. The lack of any homogenous quality among the stones, particularly in direction and grouping, produces a dynamic movement of disintegration throughout the design.

FIG. 5-14

This is a fairly static river bed, by comparison with Fig. 5-13. The channels of water force are more regular and not as strong—hence, a more homogenous grouping of the stones as a compound form. Notice the build-up of the stones behind the larger rocks, and the diminution in size of the stones as they disappear in holes in the deeper parts of the channel. This design is descriptive of forces at work and at the same time aesthetically satisfying as an image of organic compound form (growing form made up of many small units).

FIG. 5-13

FIG. 5-14

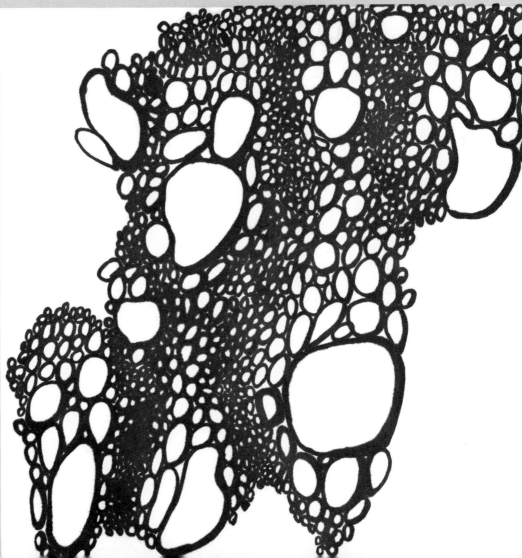

6

the intuitive organization of space

COMPOSITION NO. 10
Piet Mondrian
Here is space disturbed by marks, but unlike your experiment in making free, instinctive, brush marks in an empty space, this is tremendously organized and controlled. Where does your eye finally come to rest in this composition? Notice the subtle changes in space distribution creating a "rushing in" of the marks to one particular region. Space IV discusses how the compression of space suggests force movement.
(Rijksmuseum Kröller-Müller, Holland)

So accustomed are we to our three-dimensional world that our eyes are instinctive depth finders. In Space I (Chapter 3) when we studied the relationship between two and three dimensions, we looked at lines on a flat page and saw them in positions in depth. To further understand this natural tendency, let us consider the three main objectives of this section: (1) to establish that most of us have an instinctive or intuitive tendency to organize the placing of objects or marks in empty space, to create a seemingly "right" and organic grouping within the space available; (2) to show that we tend to see relationships between marks or objects on a piece of paper or in space, even though such marks or objects have no direct connection to each other; (3) to make a two-dimensional drawing into a three-dimensional model by taking it off the paper and giving it a three-dimensional structure in space. Three related space experiments, each one of which depends initially on an intuitive feeling for spatial relationships, will serve as a proving ground.

The first experiment is short and is intended to illustrate the instinctive tendency to distribute focal points of major and minor interest in space. Although it is extremely difficult to free the mind of all association and ideas, instinct operates so strongly in our awareness of form and space that it is possible to approach the experiment with an open mind and to allow our subconsciousness a freedom of expression. There is no doubt in my mind that knowing (by which I mean a realization in whole or in part of both the visible and the invisible) does not work only at the conscious level, but also through the mysterious channels of the subconscious mind. The artist more than anyone (except perhaps the mystic) realizes the importance of this kind of knowing.

Many people distrust the intuitive approach of some artists; others distrust an intellectual attitude. But there is really no need for suspicion on either side. Both are valid ways of knowing. Our knowledge of life is built up through both our intuition and our intellect. We should realize that they make it possible for us to make different statements about the same thing. We are always affected by the dimensions of space in which we live and in Space I we attempted to give a logical explanation of space perception. Now, let us turn to our intuitive faculties.

THE EXPERIMENTS

Experiment 1

This work has to be carried out on a sheet of white paper, not less than 20″ x 15″ in dimension, pinned to a drawing board and then erected on a semi-vertical easel at about shoulder height. You will need a regular sable water-color brush of medium size, the handle of which should be lengthened by tying it to a piece of dowel stick about 12 inches long. The lengthening of the brush handle by this means insures a lack of deliberation in handling the brush and maintains a distance between you and the paper which helps to preserve the detachment necessary for inducing an intuitive response. Now, standing at least three feet from the easel and holding the brush well at the end of the dowel stick, dip the brush into a saucer of black ink and proceed to dab the paper with the brush point. It must be stressed that there should be no attempt to *draw* with the brush: the movement should be just a touch with the point before moving back. It should be done

FIG. 6-1

An example of intuitive mark making and space filling. Focal points are made by concentrations of dabs, and depth is created by the frontal projection of dominant marks over the recession of minor ones.

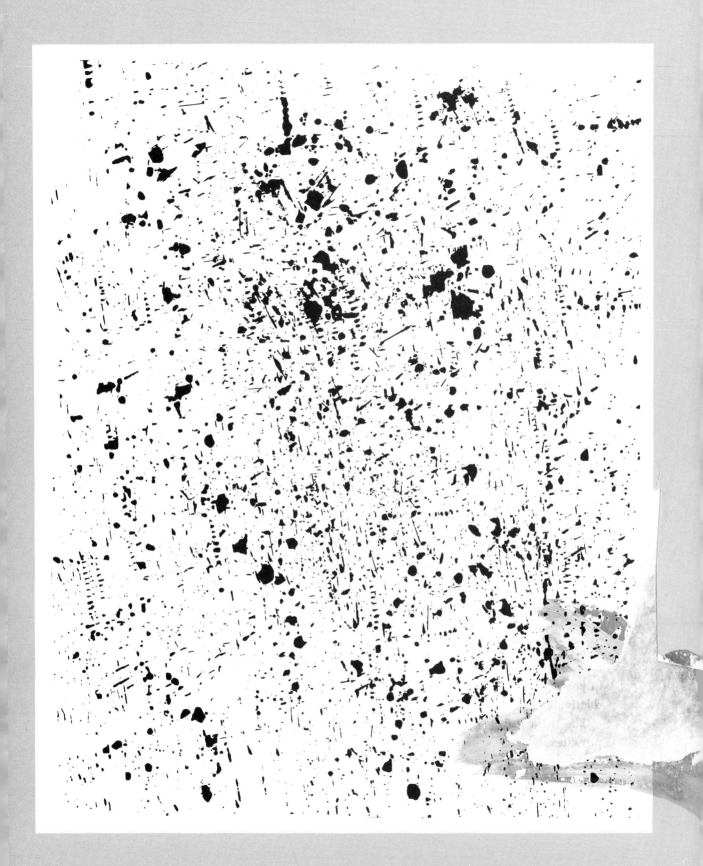

with complete relaxation, both physical and mental, the mind as complete a blank as you can make it, and the whole body loose as you move rhythmically backwards and forwards making the dabs. When there is an automatic reaction against continuing to dab, then stop. Don't think about when to stop; just stop on some such automatic impulse. Figure 6-1 is such a sheet of dab marks.

The whole thing will occupy only about three or four minutes, so when you are finished, put another piece of paper up and do another; and possibly another one after that, in order to make comparisons between the three pieces of paper which have been so marked. The first thing you will notice is that some of the dabs were made with a stronger impact than others and have produced dominant and minor marks. The differences suggest a change in strength of mechanical movements involved in making the marks, some variation in depth perception [1] as the backwards and forwards movement was repeated, and an emotional urge (present in all activity) that varied between positive and neutral degrees of stimulus as the paper space became more crowded with each new brush mark.

The second thing to be noticed if you allow your eye to wander freely over the papers is that in one or other of them your eye will probably come to rest at one particular region where there is a confluence of dabs, a concentration of dabs around one or two strong dominant marks. This represents the major focal point. (Where is the focal point in Fig. 6-2?) There may be other minor areas of concentration, or there may be no such point of concentration at all. If the marks are distributed uniformly over the total area, then the space relationships are equidistant and similar, and the eye rests nowhere. Such a regular, and therefore dull, arrangement of marks indicates a minimum intuitive ability to organize space interestingly; it also suggests that you were activated by a relatively low emotional charge.

The third and final lesson to be taken from this experiment provides a direct connection with Space I. It is that the strong black dabs project forward over the weaker gray dabs, thus making areas of depth where the eye penetrates. Now this might be accidental or still part of the whole intuitive process.

---

[1] See Space I (Chapter 3).

76

The dabs would be blacker and more powerful when the brush was newly charged with ink. The forcefulness could be related simply to the act of dipping into the ink when a purely mechanical need arose. Or one may dip in the ink to recharge the brush when he instinctively wishes for a stronger mark. But a mechanical explanation would not satisfy the question as to why certain marks should be made by flattening the brush onto the paper with some force, whereas others are the result of a delicate touch with the tip. There is a connection here with the drumbeat. A mechanical succession of beats with none louder than any other and with a regular period interval between each beat is meaningless. Only when the interval between beats is irregular and some beats are louder than others are we affected by the sound.

A number of dab experiments carried out with groups of people have indicated one thing: that in about 70 per cent of the cases, an intuitive marking of white space with black marks produced a more interesting visual result than a deliberate and conscious attempt to organize the space as a design.

Experiment 2

This work takes the previous intuitive mark-making experiment a stage further. It should produce two results: reinforcement of what has already been stated about our instinct for space organization, and an indication of how we make visual jumps of perception when faced with a scattered and random arrangement of marks in space—how we imaginatively project lines between the marks that appear significant. These lines seem to connect the marks in such a way that they form shapes on the page.

First, take a handful of variously sized pebbles and lay them out ready for easy selection. You will need another sheet of large white drawing paper, brush, and black ink. Once again attempt to relax completely; and selecting random pebbles from your collection, place them quite unself-consciously anywhere on the white paper. There is no conscious aim behind this, no particular end in view—just an instinctive putting down of the stones in the area at your disposal. As with the first experiment, don't think about when to stop; just stop when it seems right to stop. With a pencil now, draw a line around each pebble on the paper and remove the pebbles. Finally, take the brush and fill in the rings with ink.

What you now have is a collection of much larger marks, more positively shaped than the dab markings of the first experiment. Figure 6-3 is a typical example of such an instinctive pebble-placing arrangement.

This illustration reveals how well-balanced is the organization of large pebbles with smaller ones and how natural and "right" the groupings seem to be. As you continue to look, you will find that your eye tends to start at the bottom right-hand corner of the paper and move up through each pebble mark, creating an imaginary line as it does so. Your comprehension of this sheet is first a collection of black marks agreeably dispersed, but then a line is suggested moving through the marks and pulling them, rather like the beads on a string, into a linear organization. This effect is similar to the fascination of joining dots with lines that one experienced at a younger age with children's puzzles. The eye is always ready to be led onwards, particularly when new and interesting changes of direction are suggested by the next jump. A distribution of marks thus leads the eye and the imagination a merry dance—perhaps from a starting point to a finishing point, or perhaps to no definite end at all but just in a perpetual movement. The fact remains, however, that our eye is led over surfaces through points of emphasis and points of directional change. This is true as well for the surface of a canvas or the wall of a building (see Fig. 6-4). The eye also sees the marks in depth by assessing their relative degrees of darkness and size. Obviously, then, the placing of accents (dominant marks) by the artist or designer, the child drawing, or the housewife placing furniture over a floor area greatly affects our perception of the total space involved (Fig. 6-1).[2] Dominant marks also guide our perception of the linear relationships between units that occupy the space (Fig. 6-3).

For evidence that an instinctive attitude in placing the marks in space produces results aesthetically[3] superior to those placed through a conscious attitude, see Fig. 6-5.

----

[2] Chapter 12, "Form and Space," points out that we are not aware of space until it is identified by form acting as a marker buoy.

[3] See Form III (Chapter 5) for an understanding of the word "aesthetic."

FIG. 6-2

COMPOSITION NO. 10

FIG. 6-3

Sheet recording the non-deliberate placing of pebbles.

FIG. 6-4

FAÇADE, PALAZZO FARNESE, ROME (1530-1548) Sangallo and Michelangelo, architects. *Horizontal divisions created over a wall surface. One's eye jumps along the top of the window pediments, bridging the gaps between and thus creating horizontal lines which make proportionate divisions of the total wall surface. (Photograph by Alinari)*

FIG. 6-5

Sheet recording the deliberate, "design-conscious" placing of pebbles and the commonplace result.

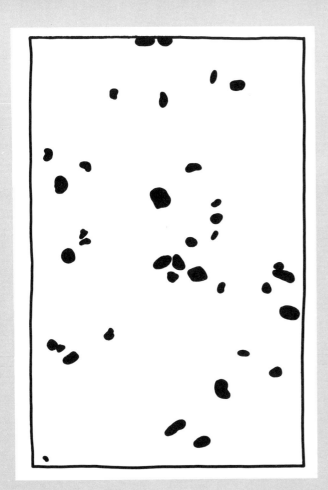

FIG. 6-3

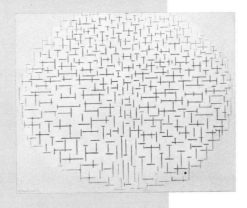

FIG. 6-2

FIG. 6-4

FIG. 6-5

This illustration shows what often happens when the student is told to arrange the pebbles in as pleasing and rhythmical a way as he can, utilizing the space at his disposal to the best possible advantage. This illustration shows an obviously contrived attempt to be decorative and to suggest movement. It is highly derivative from plant form, and there is no mystery about the form the pebble marks suggest as the eye connects them into a line of drawing. In contrast, the intuitive organization of Fig. 6-3 allows the eye to wander in and out of possible combinations of linear connection, always changing and at differing depth levels of three-dimensional suggestion. These two illustrations provide a good example of how the instinctive judgment is often better than the calculated decision.

Experiment 3

To round out this section dealing with the intuitive appreciation of three-dimensional space, we shall go back to the pebble drawing of the last experiment. The problem is to translate this drawing into three-dimensional wire sculpture. It has already been pointed out that a line of drawing exists imaginatively as the eye moves from blob to blob; so draw in this line now in pencil and see what movement and form it suggests. Yet because this is a drawing on paper, this line moves in only two dimensions. (Whatever suggestions of depth or three-dimensional movement are made come through the factors discussed in Space I, Chapter 3.) But if you take a length of heavy-gauge pliable wire and attempt to reproduce in space the imaginative line passing through the pebble marks, you are actively engaged in translating this line into a true, three-dimensional environment.

This, then, is the experiment: Examine the marks of your pebbles and produce a wire sculpture in which the movement and shaping of the wire are directly inspired by the linear form which the pebble drawing suggests. Look again at Fig. 6-3, where the drawing gives the suggested line of wire sculpture only in the form of a flat silhouette. The special difficulty of this project, therefore, requires the translation of this line actually into another dimension without losing the character of the original pebble arrangement. To do this effectively demands an imaginative handling of the wire. But

FIG. 6-6

Wire models made from the pebble-placing record sheets. (Lower photograph by the instructor, Walter Wegner)

FIG. 6-7

Shell with markings from Samoa. Observe the differing size and weight of the marks, the irregular clustering of marks, and the emergence of focal points. These natural markings give considerable visual interest to the surface of the shell.

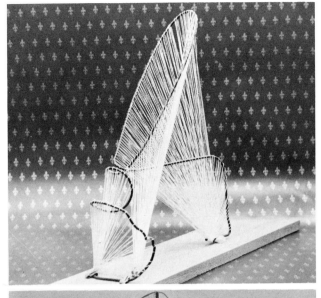

FIG. 6-6

FIG. 6-7

since all the work in this chapter has been produced so far by an immediate and therefore part-intuitive response to a situation, do not at this stage become too deliberate with the wire. Start it moving, attempt to interpret the rhythm of the pebble drawing, and be as relaxed and casual when you bend the wire into shape as you were when idly placing the pebbles on the paper. When you have finished, make some kind of heavy base to support the sculpture and then take a good look at it.

The flat line on the paper has become a line describing volume in the air. It is quite a transition from a few black marks made without thinking. But it should serve to indicate what common factors are present in all visual problems. One last thing remains to be done to complete the wire model. Pick out the planes or curved surfaces that might exist between the lines of the wire as they move in and out through space. Take some black or white cotton and by stringing up a cotton "wall" between the wires, delineate such surfaces in one or more parts of the sculpture. The finished result will resemble the models in Fig. 6-6, both of which originated from pebbles placed freely on a piece of paper. Also look at Pevsner's "Developable Column," Fig. 6-8.

This ability to translate images from one medium to another, from one dimension to another, both in imagination and in practice, is a rewarding accomplishment. It instills a knowledge of how the process of point-to-line perception works, of how important a part is played in this perception by the element of space, and of how our intuitive powers can produce space-form relationships that are aesthetically significant.

FIG. 6-8

DEVELOPABLE COLUMN (1942)
Antoine Pevsner
Brass and oxidized bronze, 20¾ inches high. Compare this sculpture with the wire forms illustrated in Fig. 6-6. Pevsner's form is doing the same thing, only in a more highly sophisticated and controlled manner. It heightens our awareness of three-dimensional regions of space and movement in these regions by its own movement out from the center and its arcing, curved surfaces. (Collection, The Museum of Modern Art, New York)

7 the conscious organization of space

The intuitive is constantly at war with the rational in the visual arts. In the previous section, the intuitive side of this struggle was discussed. Now we shall take up a "drawing" that results from logical and calculated decisions. It is true that when working freely and experimentally with no specific end in mind, one's hand is guided by intuition; but as soon as an objective problem is posed, a strong calculating attitude often takes over, and the intuition is frequently swamped. This explains why Fig. 6-5 is so commonplace. It was the response to a definite proposition put by the instructor, to which the student reacted calculatingly, and unless one has the mental powers of a Raphael, calculation can fail.

Does this mean that only the intuitive response produces art? No, it does not. But it does mean that a completely logical approach to art tends to inhibit feeling or attitude and spontaneity, which are vital to the creative process. An intellectual perfectionism devoid of these things is pretty sterile. We should strive, then, to keep our instincts alive, even when the objective is clearly stated and demands a conscious and logical application by the artist.

Here lies the reason for this experiment. It is to present a problem that will require you to think in terms of a deliberate use of space, and yet rely on the lessons of intuitive awareness

FIG. 7-1

DANCE 1
Ernest Mundt
A line in the air defining certain regions of space.
(Ernest Mundt. Associated Press News Photograph)

85

which were demonstarted in Space II (Chapter 6). The answer to the question "does only the intuitive response produce good art?" is thus that it must always be present in some degree. As you begin to explore space in this experiment, you will be required to make mental decisions, yet at the same time preserve an attitude of feeling for the spatial values your aerial construction will be creating. The necessity for the preservation of the intuitive in art is stated by Sir Herbert Read in his essay, "The Realist Heresy."

> The virtue of a symbol lies, and always did lie, in a relative degree of unintelligibility. A symbol loses its grip once its significance has been rationalized and it has become generally understood. But so long as it remains unintelligible, it can if it is a good symbol, exercise astonishing powers.

When you draw on a flat surface, your arm is restricted to making only lateral and vertical movements, and as we have seen in previous work (Space I), the third dimension of depth is introduced by the eye's innate ability to search it out—to make depth distinctions between marks and areas bounded by marks, and so on. But now we must come to grips physically with the third dimension and translate from line which bounds *area* into line which contains *volume*. See Figs. 7-1 and 7-2 for the transition from line-bounded space to volume, per se.

One way of handling space is to take a line into the air and "draw" with it. This is how the wire models of the previous section were produced. Yet wire, easily bent to produce a rhythmical cutting through space, did not demand of you any calculated decision concerning changes of direction; neither did you physically have to construct the line piece by piece when a change in direction was made. Since a strip of wood used as a line of drawing in the air does demand this greater degree of control, we will employ it in this experiment, which is to make a construction from one continuously moving line. Instead of drawing a line two-dimensionally on a flat surface, we are now going to take a line of wood strip into the air and "draw" with it three-dimensionally in space. However, before taking this line off the ground, one important stipulation has to be made: the line must move only at

FIG. 7-2

DANCE 2
Ernest Mundt
When the linear form of Fig. 7-3 revolves, the space regions become defined volumes, and the previously linear object becomes an object of volume or suggested mass. The artist's eye regarding "Dance 1" may well see the movement form of "Dance 2" without the help of motorization.
(Ernest Mundt)

right angles to itself; every time it changes direction, the angle must be 90 degrees. There are two principal reasons for this stipulation. First, it simplifies the actual making of the construction, since the wood strip, being square in section, glues together easily at a right-angle joint. Second, it will make you concentrate on proportionate lengths and three-dimensional direction. This experiment will help you see that a line moving in space creates volumes or compartments of space and that these volumes also have proportional relationships to each other and to the total construction. In addition, you should get a peculiar fascination in "drawing in depth" in the three-dimensional freedom of the air (see Fig. 7-3).

THE EXPERIMENT

The most suitable wood strip to use for this work is a balsa strip of the sort normally used in making model aircraft. About four to five feet in length is required and this should be ³⁄₁₆″ or ¼″ in section. Any of the appropriate cement fixatives will be satisfactory.

Before the line of strip wood can ascend into the air and start its wanderings, there should first be a base to support the construction, although the very ingenious construction illustrated in Fig. 7-4 balances perfectly on the single point of the first vertical length of strip. In making the base, leave it open (unconnected to its other members) at the point from which the vertical line takes off into the air. This will help the viewer establish the starting point. On leaving the base at the appropriate point, the strip should now ascend vertically into the air at right angles to the base. After this stage, you are very much on your own. It is your job now to move the strip constantly in changing directions, once it is safely airborne. Obviously, the strip will require constant support while the cement of the angle joints is hardening. But while this is happening at one part of the construction, the next few moves of the line may be seen in advance and can be prefabricated, ready to attach to the part that is drying. With every length of strip attached to the growing object, you will

FIG. 7-3

THE PALACE AT 4 A.M.
Alberto Giacometti
*Construction in wood, glass, wire, and string.
An objective organization of architectural space made by drawing with wood strip in the air. The symbolic forms are cunningly placed in their respective compartments for both meaningful and visual considerations.*
(Collection, The Museum of Modern Art, New York)

be forced ino making decisions which involve both physical and visual balance, the compartmentalization of space, and the working out of directional and angular forces. (Forces are the subjects of Form V and Space IV. In this experiment these forces may briefly be described as the tensions created in the structure by a sudden change of direction. See Fig. 7-5.) That you can now actually *see* these aspects of drawing, in handling them to put up the construction, should not blind you to the fact that the same decisions and elements exist in drawing on a flat surface.

At some point you should both think and feel that any further change of direction or further prolongation of the strip would merely confuse rather than clarify the form of the construction. Stop at this point. When completing the construction, make sure the strip line emerges into the open, so it can be seen clearly in relation to the starting point on the ground.

Conclusions

What can we learn from this experiment? Figure 7-4 provides an excellent example of a conscious working out of the problem where a feeling for space volumes and linear progression has worked hand in hand with reason. The starting point of the line can clearly be seen, and the continuation of the line through its many right-angled phases can be followed out to both finishing points. The construction has a nice asymmetrical balance, both in terms of line and volume. At the same time, as we pointed out earlier, it is also perfectly balanced physically. The thrust of line against line creates tensions in the structure of which the viewer is aware; he is also aware of the resolution of these tensions through the equilibrium achieved by the construction. Space is obviously a crucial element here. The space compartments contained within this strip drawing are organically part of the design, and they grow out of the construction; the outside space becomes a part of the drawing by entering into the construction. This interchangeability of space *contained* with space *surrounding* is an important factor, not only in the act of perceiving an object, but also in our aesthetic response to an object.

FIG. 7-4
Student wood strip construction.

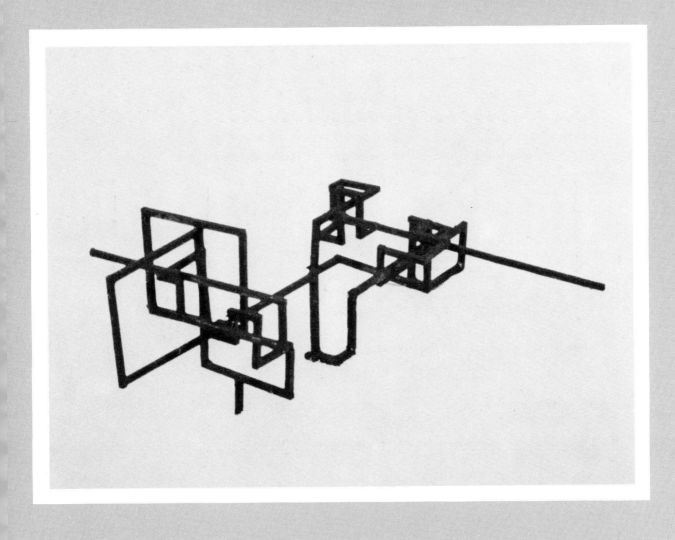

Figure 7-6 is rather different. Here there is no immediately obvious following through of the strip from its beginning to its end. Neither is there the same concern with volume or the cubic disposition of air. The student, in this case, became so interested in the visual effect created by lone, soaring lengths of line and monumental proportions, by the contrast of large rectangles with smaller ones, and by the interplay of the square and thin rectangular areas, that he took the experiment beyond the immediate class problem and produced a work of creative architectural suggestion. The fact that he ignored the rules and developed more than just one line is not really important. True, he has not created the three-dimensional drawing of Fig. 7-4, but he has done automatically what I hope many people will do *after* working through these experiments; that is, go ahead on their own and produce work which is very personal, yet based on an awareness of the structural and spatial elements involved.

FIG. 7-5

MODEL OF YORK MINSTER
CHAPTER HOUSE ROOF
On one side, the common rafters are omitted for clarity. This is a complex example of a linear construction defining space. Although the skeleton of this late thirteenth century timber roof was purely functional, the model may be enjoyed aesthetically. (Yorkshire Archaeological Society)

FIG. 7-6
Student wood strip construction.

FIG. 7-5

FIG. 7-6

8

form
in the plant:
the structural unit

We now come to a piece of work which could fit quite happily into either Part One or Part Two of this book. It is concerned with form and structure, yet also with vision and imagination. But since the basic aims underlying the experiment concern form, we rightfully should take it up here. Already we have examined the two structural families of form and the aesthetic implications of our response to form. Now we come to the stage of analyzing a particular kind of form, where search and discovery should be second nature to the inquiring eye confronted by a structure of some complexity.

It is all too often obvious, however, that not every person possesses an inquiring eye. In too many of us, curiosity, the capacity for wonder, and any sense of a personal response to the complex forms of other life in the world (Fig. 8-1), have given way to the perceptive lethargy of an automatic and mechanized civilization. Even the machines, things often of rare beauty and structure, are taken for granted by a great many people, for whom the analytical and inquiring faculty of eye fused with the imagination has become stunted.

The practice of drawing (and all the design activities that spring from drawing), makes first this demand of the eye: that it should search out objects of interest, and, concentrating, fix them in the mind that they may be more completely under-

FIG. 8-1

A sea of thistle seeds more than one foot deep. The form of the single seed, made up of delicate spiky units, can be seen in the top left-hand corner, as the seeds fall to the ground. The complexity of the ground mass, comprising several thousand identical seed-head units, cannot be described.

95

stood; thus will the imagination become active and the emotions quickened. Some of the most complex forms readily available to us, on which we can sharpen the failing powers of an inquiring eye, lie all around us in nature. Everyday things such as the dandelion seed-head, the thistle seed-head, the various types of fir cones, and the wide range of weed flowers turned to seed—these are the plant specimens to choose in order to study how the form is made up. Nature is a most efficient designer, in whose complex world of form the superfluous and the wasteful have little place. Nature is very much concerned with the *unit* of structure—with the basic part which, constantly repeated, makes up the total form. It is with this unit of structure, with the small elemental part cunningly used in a built-up system to create the whole, that this section on form is concerned (see Figs. 8-2, 8-3). The student is required to look hard at the seed form he has chosen, to select the smallest basic unit from which the complete object is built and then to use this unit in a new *structural system* to produce a new seed form. For the artist, this looking for a unit of structure becomes a habit, whether he is regarding a dandelion seed, a contemporary architectural structure (Fig. 8-4), or the honeycomb of the bee. His eye searches to discover the structural unit.

It is in the making of the final drawing demanded by this section, the drawing of the new seed form, that one very important factor about the multi-unit characteristic of form becomes apparent. For the mutation or new seed to be convincing, it must appear to be the result of organic-structural growth, rather than an apparent attempt to create an artificial novelty. It is, of course, necessary for the imagination to project from what is to what might be, but equally important is a realization of what is meant by an "organic structure," [1] by the growing, living, purposive organization of parts of a form.

THE EXPERIMENTS

Seed-head formations of plants probably provide the most complex natural objects for study, and it is possible you will

---

[1] A full explanation of organic structure is provided in the Conclusion to this section.

FIG. 8-2

The unripe pine cone showing the closed units that make up its form.

FIG. 8-3

The clematis seed structure, showing the unit organization.

FIG. 8-4

CENTRAL WASHINGTON STATE COLLEGE LIBRARY
Bassetti and Morse, Seattle, architects
Sun screen of clay tiles. Each screen is a complex honeycomb made from a small, standard unit of structure. The smaller picture shows the honeycomb units in process of construction, set up without mortar. In the background, the screens wait to receive them.
(Bassetti and Morse, Seattle. Photograph by Hugh N. Stratford)

FIG. 8-2

FIG. 8-3

FIG. 8-4

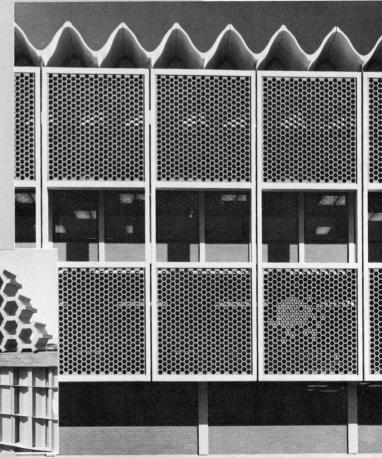

find some so complex that a magnifying glass will help in finding the unit of structure. Depending on the season, some flower formations, as well as all kinds of pond weeds and seaweeds composed of repeated units, can be found. When the chosen plant is before you, examine it closely to determine the smallest unit of structure to which it can be reduced and then extract this part and study it individually. Now on a clean sheet of drawing paper, make lots of little drawings of this unit part, with pen or pencil or wood in ink (Fig. 8-5). Make drawings from many angles until you know this part pretty thoroughly, for this is the structural unit of the plant. Drawing an object is one of the best ways to know an object. By the time you have sorted out proportions and parts from many different viewing positions, in order to describe them by drawing, you will know a great deal more than you did when you were just observing the objects.

At this stage, return to the principal object itself and examine it again. Notice particularly how the small unit attaches to the head or stem or core of the object, or even to itself. Notice the regularity of the pattern of attachment, the point of attachment, the angle of attachment, and so on. When you are fairly confident that you understand how the complete object works, both structurally and organically, make a drawing of the complete seed-head or plant. This drawing will be the more convincing because of your analytical observation. Such a drawing need not be fine enough to illustrate a nature book, but just an honest and direct result of observation and an awareness of how the thing is made. The illustrations indicate the variety of approaches students will make to this procedure of analysis through drawing. If you look at Figs. 8-6 to 8-10 you will see the stages through which such analytical probing moves. Figure 8-6 shows the bald core of the salsify seed head; in 8-7, the student is assembling the parts onto the core, and in 8-8 the unit-complex structure is complete. Then under further observation, this large complex is broken down into a dispersal of points in Fig. 8-9, eventually to become a disintegrating series of point forces in Fig. 8-10. Yet in this last drawing, notice how even the furthermost points are still dynamically retained by the center nucleus; they are still part

FIG. 8-5

Drawing notes made at random as a student begins to dissect several natural objects.

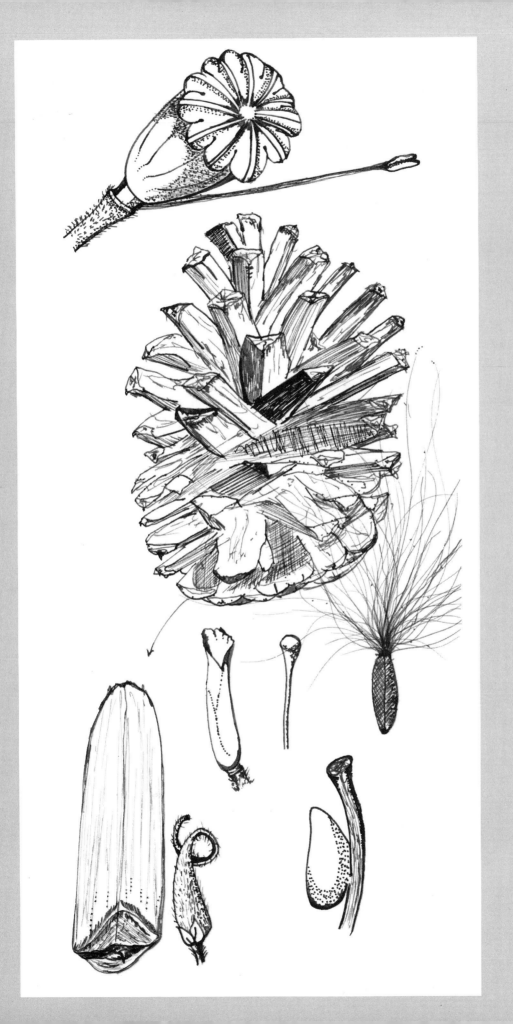

of the system, and one senses that no further disintegration will occur. This final drawing has become an abstract dispersal of points, yet it must be understood that such an accurate simplification can be achieved only when the artist knows the "how" of the seed, after analytical surgery through drawing. You now have made drawings of the unit of structure and of the major object itself. To produce them, you had, in fact, to be a surgeon—to take to pieces and then build up again. Now with this knowledge of the *parts* and of the *whole*, you are asked to use your imaginative ability to design a new plant form. You must take the small unit of structure and by inventing a *new grouping system* of the parts, a *new organization of structural pattern* having its own principles of attachment and directional movement, produce a new total object. This new object will be a variant from the original, the kind of object not yet seen in nature, but which could be produced by some interference with the biological laws governing heredity and growth—in other words, a mutation or new development (see Figs. 8-11 to 8-16).

Conclusions

Many of the obvious conclusions to be drawn from this work have already been stated in advance, both in the introduction to this section and in the description of the project itself. But always when a task of this kind is completed, one or two factors loom up large and clear as the most important aspects of it to remember. In this case a clue is provided by the three words used earlier in the final paragraph of the Introduction, the phrase "organic structural growth." The implication of the word "organic" is one of a living condition or a systematic, nonaccidental organization of parts. The dandelion and the fir cone are living objects, and their parts consequently are structured in an organic way. Our perception of these objects as "living" and "growing" is assisted by this organic structural organization. Take an object like a steel desk, which has not arrived at its final shape through the living, growing process of the repetition of a structural unit or cell, and we perceive it as an inanimate object, artificially made.

By far the greatest problem you had in creating your

FIG. 8-6

The bald core of the salsify seed-head.

FIG. 8-7

Assembling the structural units onto the bald core.

FIG. 8-8

The complex unit structure of the salsify seed-head, complete.

FIG. 8-9

The abstract dispersal of points of the seed-head.

FIG. 8-10

The seed-head reduced to a disintegrated series of point forces.

FIG. 8-6

FIG. 8-7

FIG. 8-8

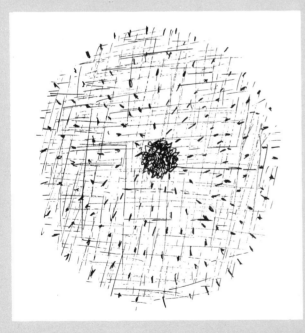

FIG. 8-9

FIG. 8-10

mutation lay in the organization of the new structural pattern, using the old structural unit, because—at the end of it all—your new plant form would either appear artificial and incapable of life or it would be as believable an organic structure as the original object.

The deduction to be made from this is that your early analysis of the plant should contain an appreciation of its organic element, for such an appreciation is part of one's aesthetic response to this kind of object. Such an appreciation would be sensitive to the rhythmic structural relationship of part to part and of all the parts to the complete form. Such a relationship of parts does not necessarily imply a mathematical or geometric regularity of structural organization although this is how the Greeks understood it (see Fig. 8-17, Greek vase about 650 B.C.). The structure can be completely irregular and curvilinear to a degree or angular to a degree, yet still possess an organic structural growth.

If you were concerned with designing a chair to be made completely from wood, you probably would try, consciously or otherwise, to make the legs belong structurally to the seat, to make the back grow from the seat—and to give both back and legs some relationship, some kinship which is imparted to them through an organic rhythm or sense of living structure.

A chair design which is just "thrown together," the parts at sixes and sevens with each other, will appear ludicrous by comparison and quite unconvincing. The dissection of the original plant form to its basic unit of structure helped to reveal its organic growth pattern. This was the purpose of suggesting such an analysis.

There are, of course, relationships between the parts of an object or the parts of a design which are not organic in the living, growing sense, but depend upon other associational elements such as a common scale, a suggested equal weight, a common color, or something of this kind. In painting, for example, such relationships may be more important than any sense of organic structure. But I think it is true to say that as soon as one becomes concerned with the object existing in space as a three-dimensional form, then the organic sense of its parts is one of the fundamental appraisals we give it—one might almost say "that we demand of it."

FIG. 8-11

The natural pine cone in its ripe, open state.

FIG. 8-12

The extracted unit of structure.

FIG. 8-13

The cone mutation. The tight clustering of the units around a central nucleus or core is in direct contrast to the horizontal stratification of the ripe and open cone. By comparison, one feels the tightness of the units in the mutation. It would not be easy to pry one away, as in the natural object.

FIG. 8-14

The complex of nuclei and trailing threads of the wild cottonseed formations.

FIG. 8-15

The extracted unit of nucleus and threads.

FIG. 8-16

The mutation or new plant form. This has been accomplished by grouping several nuclei together into a centrally organized motif, thus producing this comparatively regular, radial structure.

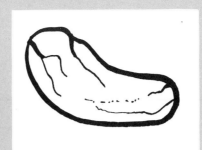

FIG. 8-12

FIG. 8-13

FIG. 8-11

FIG. 8-14

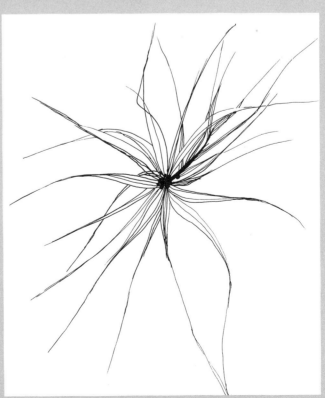

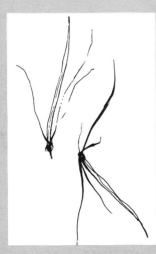

FIG. 8-15

FIG. 8-16

The study, through drawing, of the unit-structure type of natural object, focuses our attention on its smallest unit, providing we are prepared to probe and analyze it sufficiently. When we know about the small unit, we know about the whole. It is important that we are able to understand and recognize that kind of form which is made up of a multiplicity of small repeating parts and see the significance of this kind of structure for the architect, the industrial designer, and anyone concerned with building a structure in space.

FIG. 8-17

GREEK AMPHORA
(675-650 B.C.)
The complete symmetry and logical regularity of this ceramic form makes a calculated appeal to the intellect. This is how the Greeks understood structure and form, through a system of harmonious linear and area relationships—a refined and perfect structural geometry.
(The Metropolitan Museum of Art, New York)

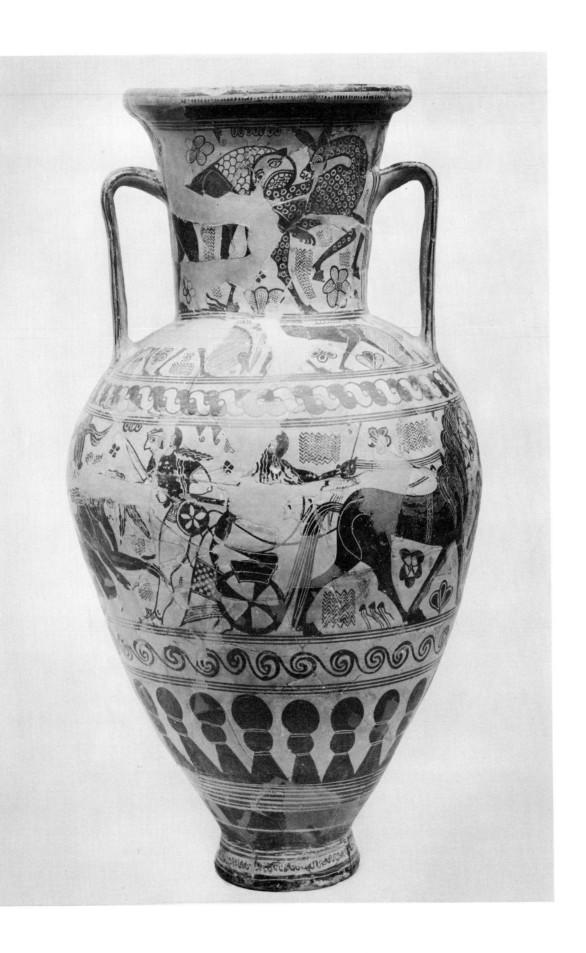

9

planes
and curved surfaces:
forces and surface tension

PHILLIPS PAVILION, BRUSSELS
INTERNATIONAL EXHIBITION
(1958)
Le Corbusier, architect
*Like a huge piece of tent
cloth, the folds of this structure are organized around the
points of force, the gigantic
"tent poles" from which the
walls are suspended.*
(The Architectural Review,
London)

Before proceeding through this chapter we should briefly re-
capitulate the aspects of form previously touched upon. We
started by defining two structural families of form, then discovered something about a person's reactions to form in terms
of what was called an "aesthetic response." After this, plant life
came in for examination, so that we might see how the repetition of a unit makes up a complete form of organic significance.
Now we shall move into the wide-spreading regions of space,
into landscape and architecture, where our attention is not
focused on the single, free-standing object, but explores ex-
pansive areas of surface. Nevertheless, the principles discussed,
which are of forces and pressures affecting the surface organization of form, apply equally to the smaller, individual object,
but they can best be studied in landscape, in the spreading
surface of the earth in its movements from mountain to valley.
Similarly, when standing within the gracious space-sculpture
of much contemporary architecture, we are led visually
through organizations of undulating wall movement and
sweeps of ceiling, with surface movement on a grand scale
taking us through large areas of space. The surface aspect of
form is not perceived at any one single point of focus, but the
eye skates over varying directional surfaces, to be bounded in
landscape only by a horizon. And in architecture which some-

times appears to have no bounds at all, wall and ceiling surfaces move out and then return to their source in an apparently self-perpetuating system (see Fig. 11-3).

So now we move from the object in isolation to the motion of the continuous surface of the sea, of the land, and of architecture—we move, in fact, to the surface of form.

This aspect of form is concerned with planes and curved surfaces, with the external aspects of form, with the constant movement of surface as the shape is revealed. Altogether in this book there are six chapters on form dealing with fundamental issues of which every student of art should be aware. In addition, of course, there are other important aspects of form not dealt with here, and a book about them all would be a very thick volume.

If you put your mind to imagining "landscape" for a moment, you will realize that the surface movement just described can be of two kinds. It can be gentle and curvaceous or sharp and angular—gentle *folds* or crevicelike *angles*—the rolling countryside or the precipitous mountain. And in architecture, too, these same kinds of surface movement occur. It is therefore possible to make two general statements about surface movement: that it is (1) a series of multi-directional planes producing through their juxtaposition an *angular* surface quality where plane meets plane; and (2) an undulation of curved surfaces producing a *folded* surface quality. It is, of course, possible to find both types of surface side-by-side in the same form, the sharp angle and its plane giving way to the fold with its curve. Architects, particularly, make use of this sudden transition of surface movement.

The work which this section is now going to propose makes a definite statement. It suggests that the folds and angles of a crumpled piece of paper have a direct relationship to the planes and curves of the earth in landscape and to the planes and curves of surfaces in architecture. The fact that the scale of a crumpled piece of paper is so much smaller than that of a mountainside or the dome of a cathedral is no objection to this proposition. Scale is not relevant because the degree of commonality in other ways is so pronounced—the common characteristics of surface plane and surface curvature shared by forms, irrespective of their relative sizes. For example, if a photograph of the crumpled paper were to have a part of it

FIG. 9-1

Grooves formed in the soft sand by the action of the incoming tide. An interesting illustration of surface formation resulting from the operation of forces.

greatly magnified, it would appear perfectly credible as an aerial view of a mountain range. The planes, angles, and valleys of the paper are only a smaller version of the surface characteristics of mountain terrain. This is rather an important point: the realization that all surface formations are made up of planes in juxtaposition or curved surfaces in series, either separately or together, and that it is only in scale that differences occur. No other formations of surface exist. So once again for the artist, the minutiae of form are as important as the monumental, and a study of the surface of the one yields information about the surface organization of the other. Hence, the crumpled piece of paper can become Mount Everest or the folds in the lay of the land. *The surface of the form*—this is our concern in the drawing experiment of this section. But before moving on to a description of the work, another important aspect of surface organization must be described. The surface of form is merely an indication of operating forces (see Fig. 9-1).

If one allows one's eye merely to play over the planes and curves, without at the same time sensing the forces that have worked within the form or pressed upon it, then he loses the complete significance of plane and curve as the surface manifestation of force or tension to which the mass is subject (see Fig. 9-2).

This then is the implication of the words "structural organization" as applied to surface. The word "organization" is used to imply that the surface of form takes the shape it does because of the forces exerted on it, either from within or without. For example, if one attempts to straighten out a piece of curved bark, the surface detail of the bark will change its formation. Or think of it another way: if one drapes a piece of material over the top of a vertical pole, the resulting folds are organized by virtue of the vertical point-thrust beneath; but if one drapes the same material over the seat of a chair, then there will result quite a different organization of surface fold because the resistant pressure force beneath is a different kind of pressure. As another example, take a flat sheet of aluminum which, lying on the table, constitutes a plane surface and which, held vertically, is still a plane surface. But if mechanical force is exerted to pull the two sides round together, then the aluminum sheet is no longer a plane surface, but a curved surface.

FIG. 9-2

WOMAN COMBING HER HAIR
Alexander Archipenko
A sculpture of planes and angles, curved surfaces, depressions and protrusions. As the surface of the crumpled paper represents the pressure exerted, so does the surface organization of this sculpture represent the artist's forceful shaping of his medium into the pressure forms of the human figure. The point thrust and pressure thrust which are described in Space IV (Chapter 11) play an important part in Archipenko's dynamic abstraction of the figure.
(Collection, The Museum of Modern Art, New York)

The stronger the force applied, *the more apparent is the tension over the surface of the curve.*[1] Surface tension is thus greater over any curved surface than over any plane surface, and the more pronounced the curve, the more surface tension is induced. From this it will be seen that when eventually a curve becomes an angle (as it does with the aluminum sheet if great force continues to be exerted at the sides), then the surface tension over the *angle* is very considerable. Hence, skin stretched tight over projecting bones has considerable surface tension as it changes direction. This is why skeletal-form surfaces are more dramatic than gently curving bulbous-form surfaces. The surface tension is both seen and felt by the viewer (see Fig. 9-3).

In landscape, the earth has been worked on by forces—internal and external—and the surface form we see is the present *status quo* achieved by these forces. The architect achieves equilibrium in a building through the interaction of forces, through the pressure force of roof against wall, wall against foundations, and so on. Sometimes the tension of his surfaces is indicative of the operation of these forces (see Fig. 9-4). When a mountain is drawn by a man who both sees and feels the surface to be a manifestation of the forces that shaped the earth, then he produces a dramatically revealing statement about "mountain." To see this, look at John Piper's "Slope of Tryfan" (Fig. 9-5). Yet when another man merely draws the surface appearance of the mountain without equating this with the forces that shaped it, then all we have is a piece of stage scenery.

THE EXPERIMENT

First, select two pieces of paper, each one about 2' square, one a crisp, strong paper and the other a soft, absorbent paper. Using both hands, deliberately crumple up each piece separately, not so strongly that you reduce it to a small and formless ball, but with just enough strength to produce a complex of planes, angles, and folds. With this accomplished, you now have some personal experience of force being responsible for surface organization. At the same time, you will notice a difference between the crumpled papers. The strong paper will have

[1] Surface tension is the result of forces in opposition, the molecular forces of the substance versus the mechanical forces exerted on it.

FIG. 9-3

WOMAN'S HEAD (1909)
Pablo Picasso
*Bronze, 16¼ inches high.
The cubist tendencies of this sculpture give a pronounced emphasis to the planes and curved surfaces of the head. Structure is dominant, and the sharply formed angles produce a surface tension which heightens the dramatic quality of the form.
(Collection, The Museum of Modern Art, New York. Purchase)*

FIG. 9-4

PHILLIPS PAVILION

FIG. 9-5

SLOPE OF TRYFAN (1950)
John Piper
*A mountain drawn by a man who sees the planes and curves of the form's surface as a manifestation of the forces that shaped the earth.
(John Piper)*

FIG. 9-3

FIG. 9-4

FIG. 9-5

formed sharply defined planes and clean angles; the soft paper will be altogether more "blurred," less angular, and with a suggestion of curved surfaces rather than planes. This difference is due to the varying resistance that the paper offers the pressure. After seeing this, we are now in a position to make a further generalization about the formation of surface planes and curves: *the stronger and more rigid the material, the sharper will be its angles and the more distinct its planes when forces operate to shape the form.* For the softer, less rigid materials, the converse is true. Hence, soft fabric under such conditions develops a surface that is curved and folded rather than planed and angular.

Two drawings of each crumpled paper form have now to be made. Choose your own drawing medium for this. The first drawing of each piece of paper is to be entirely a line drawing (Fig. 9-6). This will be an attempt to describe the surface formation of the angles and planes of the crisp, strong paper form, followed by the folds and curved surfaces of the soft paper form. The second drawing of each piece of paper is to dispense with line altogether. Half-close your eyes and see the form as an organization of surface areas (planes or curves) *but do not look for their edges.* Now, using shading or tone, build up the form, bit by bit, by "blocking in" with tone each plane area or curved area over the whole shape—rather like building up piece by piece with bricks (Fig. 9-7). Any lines or edges that are formed will occur automatically where the tone shading stops or changes intensity (Fig. 9-8). The dark or light quality of the tone should be taken directly from the objects. Where the planes or curves appear lighter or darker, adjust your tone shading to a similar intensity. If a pen is being used, then tone is best indicated by lines, heavy or light, closely concentrated or widely spread across the face of the plane or curve (Fig. 9-9). With these four drawings complete, some conclusions should now be made, conclusions which add more to our knowledge of the surface organization of form and which suggest the importance for the artist of an awareness of forces and tensions when he is faced by surface movement of plane and curve.

Conclusions

The carefully crumpled piece of paper is no simple form; and when one has the task of drawing it, deciding where to start is

FIG. 9-6

Line drawings with pen and pencil of a crumpled piece of hard paper. Both drawings are well-observed expressions of the form with its complicated surface of planes and curves produced by the crumpling force. Points 1 and 2 made in the Conclusion to Form V are borne out in these drawings.

FIG. 9-7

The crumpled paper is built up through areas of tone, with each plane acting rather like a chunk of masonry. Any linear quality is merely the result of changes in tonal intensity. This form is credible as a piece of paper, a large piece of rock, or an aerial view of a range of hills.

FIG. 9-6

FIG. 9-7

a difficult decision. As the eye searches the surface, moving from plane to plane and angle to angle, the mind is also working along with the eye, trying to relate the surface to forces in the form pushing out and forces from outside the form pushing in; for in crumpling the paper, a thumb might have pushed in, while a finger pushed out.

The statement has been made elsewhere in this book that drawing is a way to knowledge, that looking with intent increases our understanding of form, and the quality of our attitude to it. This applies perfectly to these pieces of crumpled paper. After drawing them, the following facts about the structural organization of their planes, angles, curves, and folds are apparent.

1. Surface planes and curves tend to be organized two, three, or more to a group, and planes or curves in the same group all tend to emanate from a single point. The arrangement can be seen by following the angle lines through to a group source. It is fairly obvious what this point is: it is the point of force operating internally or externally on the form. Think again of the cloth over the vertical pole: all the folds will originate from the point of suspension or pushing-up force. So a plane with its angles does not exist alone on a multi-directional surface. It is organized with other planes, angles, and curved surfaces about a point of force. If this is not understood in a drawing, then this special relationship between the surface of the form and the forces that have operated to shape it will not be conveyed, and the drawing will not convince.[2]

2. The material of the form will tend to move either vertically or laterally until it meets an opposing directional movement occasioned by a second and different force. To take the example of the cloth over the vertical pole once more, the folds of this material hang vertically throughout the whole length of the material, and no horizontal folds run contrary to them. But as soon as the cloth is supported at a second point—say halfway down, by placing an arm beneath it—then a horizontal movement develops which interrupts the sweep of the vertical. Thus a connection between points of force is to be found in the opposing horizontal and vertical movements of the planes

FIG. 9-8

Two carefully analyzed paper forms. Elimination of some detail reveals the organization of the folds around points of force. The dotted-line technique permits a conscious visual probing of the form while drawing and also prevents too strong a concentration on the edge of the form.

FIG. 9-9

In this drawing of a crumpled piece of soft paper, the tone is produced by lines rather than by "shading." The contour line lends itself to the drawing of varied surface movement and, for this student, is a legacy from Form II (Chapter 4). It could easily become a mechanical cliché if used indiscriminately. Each drawing problem should suggest its own method of expression and technical solution.

---

[2] Students' still-life drawings and paintings, in which plane and curved surfaces abound, often fail to show an awareness of surface relationships that result from the forces at work. This is particularly true of draped fabrics, folded papers, etc.

FIG. 9-8

FIG. 9-9

or curves. The vertical movement has the upper hand, since the force of gravity constantly pulls the material in a downward direction.

This scheme of vertical plane, opposed and met by horizontal plane, can be seen in the crumpled paper or on the mountainside. In architecture, the same principle is observed where the horizontal ceiling meets the vertical wall. As long as the forces are roughly equal in strength and capable of being contained by the material (the paper did not disintegrate under the forces exerted upon it), then equilibrium results. The crumpled paper represents an organization of planes and curved surfaces in vertical and lateral opposition, yet in a state of stability rather than disintegration.

The final experiment

To see how you retain all this theory and use it in a project which deals with the organization of surface, let us tackle an imaginative problem of surface design. Using pen or pencil, line or tone, make a drawing of a strange and fantastic rock surface. It can be cliff or free-standing rock; it can be composed of planes or curved surfaces; it can be stratified horizontally, vertically, or in both directions. To do this you may wish to work from the crumpled paper, using it as a stimulus for an imaginative projection involving expression or distortion; or you may just sit down and let the surfaces and their shaping forces take over and grow on the paper imaginatively. Either way, you should now have enough background knowledge to work confidently. The proof will be in the drawings, which will indicate how strongly you have felt and expressed "force" as the cause of surface structure. See Fig. 9-10 as an illustration of this imaginative surface design.

FIG. 9-10

The crumpled paper becomes the imagined mountain range. All the knowledge gained from the study of planes, curved surfaces, and forces has gone into this drawing.

FIG. 9-11

Surface organization of the underside of the mushroom. The vertical planes with their sharp edges could be simulated with sharply folded paper.

FIG. 9-10

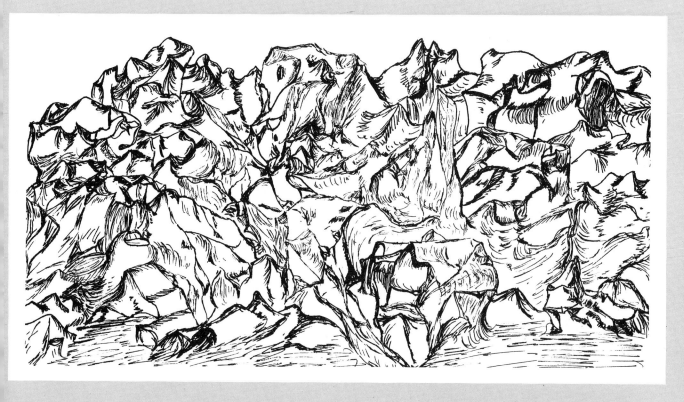

FIG. 9-11

10

surface

texture

There is a tremendous interrelationship between the visual sense and the tactile sense, between *looking* and *touching*. More than once we have drawn attention to one's ability to "feel" an object imaginatively with one's fingertips, merely by looking hard at it. This interrelationship probably exists among all the five senses; for example, a particular smell will create in the mind's eye an image of the object associated with it. But sight and touch, especially, have this power to stimulate each other.

Any study of form would be incomplete without some discussion of "touch" quality—of its hardness or softness, dryness or dampness, smoothness or roughness, and so on. This aspect of form is most often revealed by its surface texture. In the work just completed, dealing with surface structure, little reference was made to texture, although it vitally affects our reaction to form. Strongly contrasting textures have considerable power to arouse a strong aesthetic response—attraction or repulsion. Think of a smooth stone half-covered by a soft growth of moss; or an apple smooth and shiny on top but soft, rotten, and fungus-covered on the bottom; or the skin of a woman's face against the texture of a fur collar; or silk stockings in contrast to woolen ones; or, finally, imagine drinking cold milk from a fur-lined bottle. The list could be continued indefinitely. Contrasting textures act as contrasting colors: they complement each other or heighten our awareness of their differing quality.

The architect, the sculptor, the designer in industry, and the painter—all use surface textures to capitalize on the sensitive relationship between sight and touch. An immediate question arises: how effective is an artificially contrived texture when compared with the natural texture of a material? Although we ask the question here specifically about surface texture, this issue of the contrived versus the natural has wide ramifications in the field of art. We would suggest this answer to the specific question: when the surface treatment of a material disguises the true nature of the material, then the aesthetic possibilities of the surface are reduced rather than enhanced.

Examples of such falsification abound in the history of art and design. When the baroque style of architecture was at its summit in eighteenth-century Europe, wood and plaster were skillfully treated to resemble marble, bronze, gold, or silver (see Fig. 11-3, the church of "Die Wies" in Bavaria). The immediate effect on entering the church is wonderful. But as one moves in and touches a "marble" column, it is not cold, crystalline, and smooth; it feels of wood, and immediately something is wrong. The total effect of the building still remains a delight, but it cannot be enjoyed intimately and lovingly through knowledge of its detail. An aesthetic flaw remains.[1]

Some materials possess an unattractive surface quality. Plaster is one. There are things one can do to plaster to enhance its textural quality, but it should never be falsified to resemble some other material. Most artists try to choose a material for its natural surface texture, and they interfere with it little. The art lies in the selection rather than in excessive interference. When the painter uses water color, he wants its transparent, limpid softness; when the architect stipulates concrete, he wants its surface quality in his design [2] (see Fig. 10-1).

The following experiments are intended to bring the student into firsthand contact with surfaces—to involve him in looking and selection, then in the actual touching of the surface, and finally in representing surface textures through drawing.

---

[1] For a fuller understanding of why this should be so, read again the description of aesthetic implication in Form III (Chapter 5) with its suggestion of "completeness" or realization of "truth."

[2] Obviously, structural reasons for choosing concrete may be more important than surface requirements.

FIG. 10-2

Sheet of collected surface rubbings, mounted to show a range of varied textures.

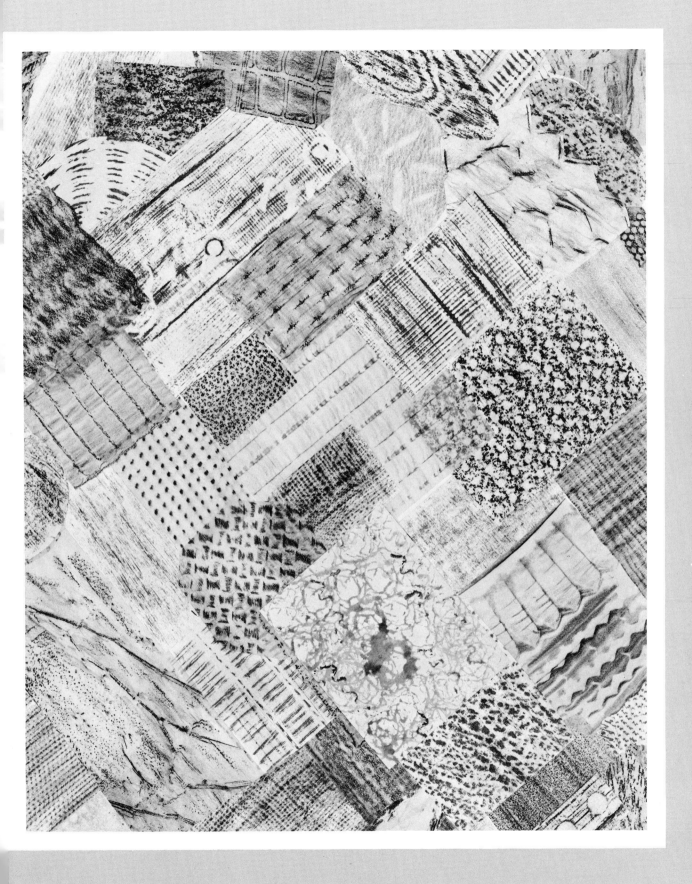

THE EXPERIMENTS

For the first part of this work you will need a large, soft drawing pencil or a large, black grease crayon, together with some small sheets of tracing paper. (Any reasonably strong semi-transparent paper will do.) For the next hour or so, attune your eye toward a sensitivity for surfaces, both indoors and out: wood, metal, plastic, concrete, textiles, bricks, rocks, leaves, skins—any surface that excites the eye and imaginatively activates the touch sense. From each surface take a rubbing of a small area (about 3″ x 3″); use the tracing paper and the soft lead or grease pencil, so that you produce a graphic simulation of the surface quality of the material. When you have some thirty of these, gather them all together, trim down the edges of each piece, and mount them all together on a large sheet of paper. The result will be something like Fig. 10-2, which incorporates rubbings ranging from an auto tire to an iron-stranded cable, to a loaf of bread.

The second part of the experiment is to select three of these mounted rubbings in order of visual dominance—that is, select the texture which stands out from the rest by virtue of its intensity of black and vitality of surface. Then choose a texture that is neither very dominant nor very weak—a middle distance texture. Finally, pick out the most unobtrusive texture, the surface that recedes more than any other in the collection.

Having made these selections, reproduce the three textures in a drawing, remembering the means by which a variety of drawing marks was produced in Chapter 2 (Fig. 2-1). In order to put the textures "in their place," make a rectangle approximately 9″ x 6″ and divide it by means of three lines into four areas. Let this division be freely executed, the lines forming a natural, twiglike skeletal structure. This will give you space division of an irregular, curvilinear quality like the rectangle-enclosed skeletal drawings of Form I (Chapter 1) especially if the dividing lines are not of equal weight. In that division of the rectangle which appears most frontal,[3] reproduce the dominant texture just selected, using any drawing or mark-making means. The texture should fill the area completely. Follow this

---

[3] See Space I (Chapter 3), areas enclosed or bounded by lines of differing weight and quality.

FIG. 10-3

Textures produced by drawing. The three textures were selected in each case from the sheet of mounted rubbings and were to suggest three depth levels when placed together in a diagram.

FIG. 10-4

Strange textures given to familiar objects. Are they any longer objects to eat or to touch?

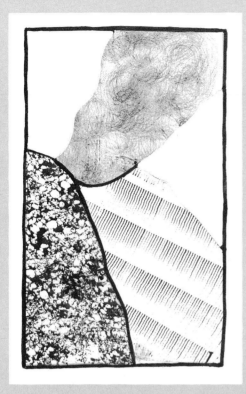

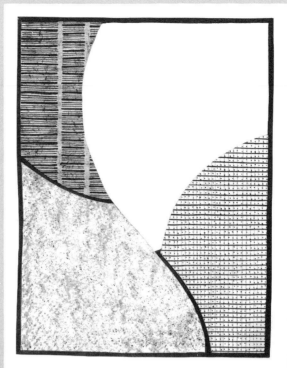

FIG. 10-3

FIG. 10-4

by reproducing the moderately strong texture in the middle distance division of the rectangle, and then draw the meekest texture in any other division of the rectangle. For purposes of contrast, one area in the rectangle will be empty, both texturally and spatially. Black drawing ink is the best medium to use, with pen, wood, dry brush, piece of sponge or any other effective instrument. Figure 10-3 shows two illustrations of textures that have been skillfully simulated through such drawing. They also indicate the degree of immediacy or partial recession which textures in this kind of spatial context possess.

Finally, as an imaginative exercise, let us see what strange and mysterious effects are produced when a familiar form is given an unfamiliar texture. Make a series of small drawings of objects with which you are reasonably well acquainted—things like apples, faces, fish, or eggs—and invest them with a new and alien surface quality. The results appear incongruous and, on the whole, repulsive because now they possess a surrealist quality. It is the violation of the familiar that causes our repulsion, or possible attraction. But it should be sufficient indication of the importance of surface texture in determining our attitude to an object (see Figs. 10-4 and 10-5).

The cold clammy feel of a toad . . . the slimy scales of a fish . . . the silken pattern of a butterfly's wing . . . the smooth fine surface of a new potato . . . the glossy shine of white-painted walls . . . sleeping between sheets or blankets . . . the sackcloth of the penitent . . . ceramic pieces and glazes. . . . Eye, touch, and mood respond immediately to the texture of the form presented to us.

FIG. 10-5

The human eye is given an unfamiliar surface texture of scales, while the lids become speckled and strongly pored. Apart from its surrealistic suggestions, this is technically an interesting textural drawing.

FIG. 10-6

The increased visual interest created by extremes of light and shade over surfaces of uniform texture is demonstrated in this photograph. The strongly lit white stone in the middle foreground makes a dominating focal point.

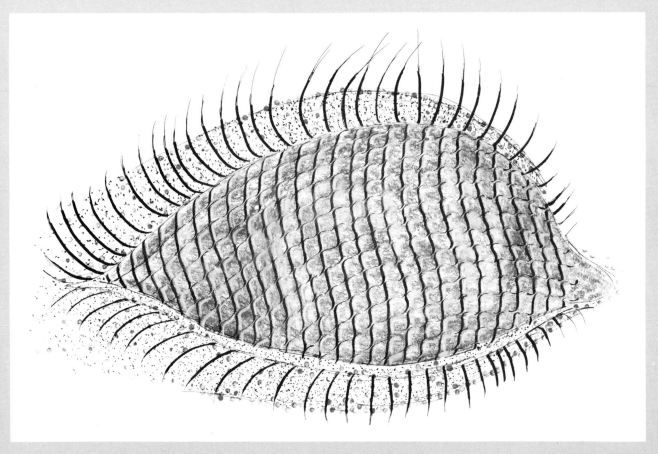

FIG. 10-5

FIG. 10-6

11

dynamic relationships:
forces,
tensions, and equilibrium

We have already had one or two previous introductions to this question of dynamic relationships between objects. For example, in the Imaginative Projects described in Form III (Chapter 5), the second of these projects asked you to consider making a drawing of a dried out, rock-strewn river bed, where large rocks and smaller pebbles lie in some kind of purposive order. The text then asked you to imagine *how* this purposive positioning was achieved—what force pushed or pulled these stones to the position they occupy—it asked you to think of the cause behind the effect, of the force of water to which the new dry stones bear silent testimony.

Before reading on, go back and have a look at Figs. 5-13 and 5-14, for these drawings provide good visual descriptions of dynamic relationships between objects—between stones, in this particular case—relationships that result from some force which has brought the objects to their present position.

Now refer back to Fig. 6-3, the drawing which was the outcome of a chance placing of pebbles on paper, where the eye jumps from one black mark to another, threading them along an imaginary line as beads on a string. Here again it is the dynamic relationship between the marks which binds them together, the directional *movement* that is suggested between mark and mark. But you will notice in this drawing that any

CHOIR VAULT, AMIENS
CATHEDRAL, FRANCE (1247)
*(Photograph by
Clarence Ward)*

129

suggestion of the force involved is weak by comparison with the river bed drawings, because space is fairly evenly distributed between the marks. As soon as space becomes compressed and the objects begin to "cluster," then an operating force becomes apparent. Hence, in the river bed drawings, the smaller stones tend to be forced in, close to the larger stones. When no space remains between them, their grouping indicates that the force was a strong one. A good illustration of such clustering is provided by the salsify seed (Fig. 8-10). Does this suggest a force of attraction to the center or a force of repulsion from the center? It could be either, but it is quite obvious from this drawing that the more *diffuse* the space becomes between the seed marks, the weaker grows the force. So a concentration of objects and a compression of space is evidence that a powerful operating force was involved (see Fig. 11-1).

We had better define some of these terms before going on to the next experiment. The word *dynamic* implies activity and movement; it is the opposite of "static." *Force* is that entity which determines the movement of mass, as the water moving the stones of the river bed, the wind blowing a tree, growth opening the leaves of a bud, or gravity attracting an object to the earth. (In the previous chapter, the word "force" was also used to describe pressures operating *in* form and *on* form, thus affecting the shape of the form.) This chapter is concerned with the dynamic aspect of things in space—with the movement or suggested movement of mass, and with pressure tensions. When several opposing forces are operating in the same region, tensions are created. Tension is simply a force opposing a force. When forces oppose each other in the parts of a building, for example, or in a rocky landscape in nature, and when they are in balance, a state of equilibric tension is achieved, or, simply equilibrium. Tensions in a state of equilibrium represent permanence and stability. When forces, because of their strengths or directions, remain unresolved and in restless opposition, the tensions created within the region, or over the form of the mass, or between the parts of the object, are not in balance and a state of nonequilibric tension or disintegration is apparent. Unstable tensions represent impermanence and instability—a fluid rather than a static situation. (Consider the tension operating over the curved surface of a bent piece of aluminum as described in the previous experiment. The tension is caused by

FIG. 11-1

Visual suggestions of movement associations (dynamic relationships) between objects in space.
(1) A regular grouping of marks and an even distribution of space, where movement suggestions between the marks are weak.
(2) An irregular grouping with an uneven distribution of space, where movement suggestion is strong, suggests a force in operation and puts each mark in a dynamic association with its neighbor.
(3) Marks affected by a centrifugal force, producing the strongest dynamic (as opposed to static) relationships.

FIG. 11-2

CHOIR VAULT, AMIENS CATHEDRAL

FIG. 11-3

PILGRIMAGE CHURCH "DIE WIES," UPPER BAVARIA (1745-1754) Dominicus Zimmermann, architect
(Photograph by Hirmer)

FIG. 11-4

The three basic forces that are used in this experiment.

FIG. 11-5

The point thrust forces of the salsify seed-head.

FIG. 11-1

FIG. 11-2

FIG. 11-3

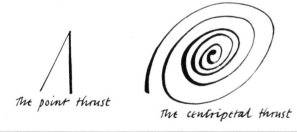

The point thrust   The centripetal thrust   The pressure thrust

FIG. 11-4

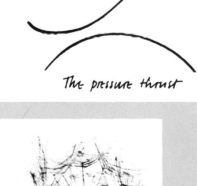

FIG. 11-5

strong mechanical forces pulling against the molecular forces of the aluminum itself—by forces in opposition. In this case, equilibrium is maintained until, in bending, the balance point between the two forces is passed, when disintegration of the aluminum sheet becomes a possibility.) A building stands because forces are in balance, creating equilibrium. A stone falls because no counterbalancing force opposes gravity.

For an example of equilibrium, look at Fig. 11-2, the choir vault of Amiens Cathedral, where the mass of the roof vault is concentrated and directed through stone ribs making a downward thrust to fixed points. These fixed points are met by the counterthrust of the vertical, up-pushing piers; and to complete the stability (although it cannot be seen in this photograph), a flying arch is thrusting in to the same point from an outside free-standing buttress. This concentration, up, down, and across to one point in the structure creates a dynamic equilibrium which is the essence of Gothic architecture. What we see are the actual structural tensions by which equilibrium is achieved undisguised by any superimposed design. For an example of a fluid, seemingly impermanent situation in architecture, see Fig. 11-3, the interior of the eighteenth-century church, "Die Wies," in Bavaria. In this baroque style of architecture the rational, precise use of forces we see at Amiens in the thirteenth century, gives way to a deliberate suggestion of a profusion of forces of varied strengths and directions, which fling the eye into a bewildering dance and give no suggestion as to how the stability of the building is achieved. The tensions suggested through the design are nonequilibric tensions, disguising the true structure. When the word "pressure" is used, it signifies forces operating in a particular way. The action of one force against an opposing force, such as a horizontal beam supported by two vertical beams, produces pressure. Pressure forces of this kind are operating in any object which is made up of a series of parts; the pressure occurs between the parts, whether the object be natural or man-made. We shall examine this aspect of form later in the chapter.

Through a system of lines, we tend to perceive the type of force that is involved in moving objects in space and the types of pressure produced in objects. We will use this system of lines to tell us what forces and pressures are at work, whether in a drawing, a piece of furniture, a plant, or a landscape. Our

FIG. 11-6

Sheet of nine free drawings exploring the possible interactions of the three given forces.

practical problem will be to make drawings in which space is disturbed by forces.

The three basic force movements that we shall use are: (1) the point thrust, (2) the centripetal thrust, and (3) the swelling pressure thrust. These three movements are illustrated in Fig. 11-4. A *point thrust* is force concentrated to one point, like a punch straight from the shoulder. A *centripetal thrust* is delivered outward from a center. For instance, a centripetal thrust produces the ripples on the surface of water when a stone is dropped, as well as the slow, uncoiling movement from the wound-up mainspring of a watch. Or imagine whirling a stone tied to a piece of string around your head. A *swelling pressure thrust* is a movement distributed over a surface, like that produced when you bend a flat piece of paper into a cylinder or expand a surface by blowing up a balloon. It is a swelling, expanding surface.

In the Gothic Cathedral of Amiens you can see an example of the point thrust, of point thrust opposing a point thrust and achieving equilibrium. The baroque church of "Die Wies," on the other hand, contains a restless suggestion of centripetal and swelling pressure thrusts, producing a feeling of tension, not equilibrium.

All three force movements are to be found in nature, sometimes operating in space—as the concentrated thrust of water over the river bed—sometimes existing singly in one object, as in Fig. 11-5, where the drawing of the salsify seed displays a concentrated point-thrust series of pressure forces comparable to those involved in the Gothic Cathedral of Amiens.

THE EXPERIMENT

One of the difficulties to be avoided in a text such as this is the danger of giving the student too rigid and dogmatic a briefing for an experiment. It is, of course, perfectly possible to make some kind of drawing or design by following a set of numbered instructions, but it is unlikely that the result will bear any of that stamp of personal awareness which is part and parcel of art. I hope that all the illustrations in this book indicate individual approaches by students who have taken the text briefing merely as a starting point. The practical work of this section is particularly difficult to describe without making too

FIG. 11-7

The selected drawing from the sheet of force explorations treated first as a line drawing and second as a black and white design. An expanding centripetal force and two point thrusts are displacing forms in the region. In five minutes, the situation could be quite different as the forces continue to operate; therefore, this could not be described as a drawing of stability.

FIG. 11-8

Two drawings where concentrated point thrusts express operating forces. In the left-hand drawing, the irresistible force meets the immovable object. The drawing on the right expresses stability or equilibrium as equal forces hold each other in balance.

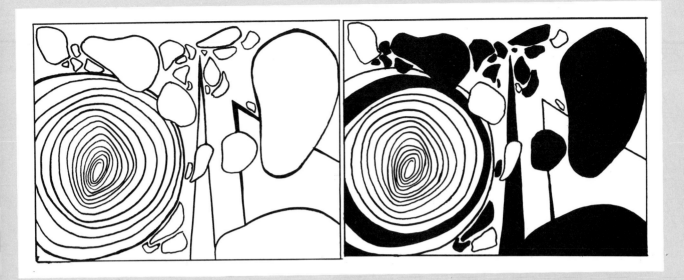

FIG. 11-7

FIG. 11-8

rigid a framework, so I shall mention here only the essentials and suggest that a study of the illustrations will yield more information than a long verbal description.

There are three parts to the work, each one dealing with different aspects of forces at work. First, using all three force movements (point, centripetal, and pressure), make a series of free drawings on one sheet of paper as in Fig. 11-6. These may be left as line drawings or may be "filled in" drawings in black and white. The problem is to contain the three different forces within the limiting size of the rectangle. Study how the space is disturbed, what direction the forces take, what the relationship is among the forces operating in the confined space, and which force dominates. Or perhaps the forces will all be equal in importance. In Fig. 11-6, the point thrust dominates in at least three of the drawings.

It is important to be very free in the manner of drawing and in the expression of the forces. Try to let yourself actually feel the type of energy they represent.

Now select from this sheet of drawings the one which conveys the most dynamic suggestion of forces and, on a larger scale, redraw this as a finished drawing, making whatever refinements you feel are necessary to intensify this feeling of energy. Make this drawing in line only, but then repeat it, blocking in areas of solid black so that you have two drawings, as in Fig. 11-7. Compare the two drawings. Which treatment helps to suggest the greatest dynamic activity, the more restless disturbance of space, and so on?

The drawings you have made so far may be drawings of equilibric tension or disintegrating tension; it depends on how you instinctively dispose the three forces. In the last stage of this work, however, produce as many drawings as you like, but with two definite aims in view: to depict forces that are in balance, creating stability, as in the Gothic Cathedral of Amiens, and forces that are in opposition, producing restless tension, as in the baroque church of "Die Wies." In making these drawings, use one type of force movement—the point thrust, for example—or use two together, or again all three. In Figs. 11-8 to 11-12, the force movements have been employed singly and together in what are essentially exploratory drawings where lines symbolizing forces in operation are used to introduce the dynamic element into drawing and design.

FIG. 11-9

A design of point thrusts aligned to fixed points in space. Movement, time, and intense concentrations of force are suggested by this drawing.

FIG. 11-10

Two drawings of forces. Notice in the drawing at the left how the three point thrusts are balanced. Only the centripetal force (caused by the intruding point force) is menacing and will eventually break through the stabilizing point force on the right. How long will this situation last? It is important to appreciate the time factor suggested in these drawings.

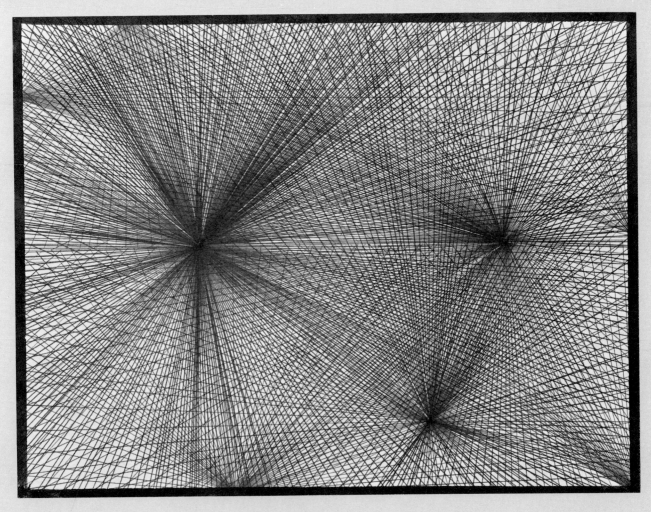

FIG. 11-9

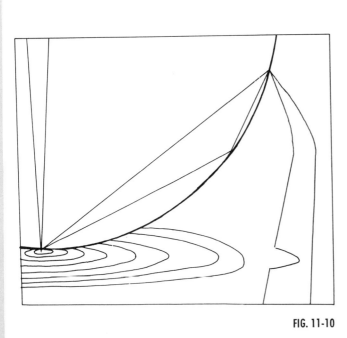

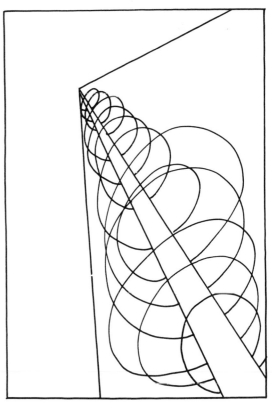

FIG. 11-10

Conclusions

First, how important are dynamic pressure relationships in the single object? Can you think of any complex object that lacks such relationships? Look at the table lamp in Fig. 11-13, for example. It is not difficult to pick out the dynamic operation of the pressure forces of its several parts. The base provides a solid and reassuring pressure thrust, giving stability. The stem with its white, inner shade produces a point thrust down to and against, the base, which is counteracted by the outer shade with its suggestion of an upward thrust away from the base. In our visual appraisal of the lamp, these dynamic suggestions profoundly influence our perception and reaction. An earlier section of the book talked about the aesthetic implications of form; now, having worked with forces, you should realize how strongly the dynamic element influences our aesthetic response. Their power was hinted at in Form V when our response to surface organization was examined, and surface was related to forces at work. Fig. 11-13 convincingly illustrates how important this dynamic connection between the parts of an object is to the industrial designer.

When we move from a single object to a group arrangement of many objects in space, the same factors hold—the suggested dynamic connection between the objects. Remember the pebble marks on the paper, and the imaginary line stringing them together? Can you imagine a living room with the furniture placed at regular, equidistant intervals, a room with no focal points? It rarely happens. Or a landscape where tree, rock, river and mountain are all disposed in a perfect geometric order repeated ad infinitum as far as the eye can see. Impossible. But if it were so, we would work to push some boulders into a group, fell a few trees to break the pattern—anything to introduce dynamic tension, the result of operating forces, into the situation. In nature, rock thrusts against rock; the river scours its resistant banks; trees and plants thrust up into the sky; air currents whirl around; all is in a state of tension, a state of dynamic expansion (growth) and contraction (decay). This is not the unchanging equilibrium of forces, the perfect balance of forces of the Cathedral of Amiens—nature knows no such stability (Fig. 11-14). As in nature, so in art. No work of art can be completely devoid of some dynamic quality; although,

FIG. 11-11

Two drawings of forces of intrusion where a foreign body is exerting pressure on, or in, a substance. The result is tension, due to the lack of balance between the forces, and ultimately, perhaps, disintegration of the substance.

FIG. 11-12

Three drawings of forces expressing movement and pressure. Only the lower right drawing suggests a fairly permanent situation.

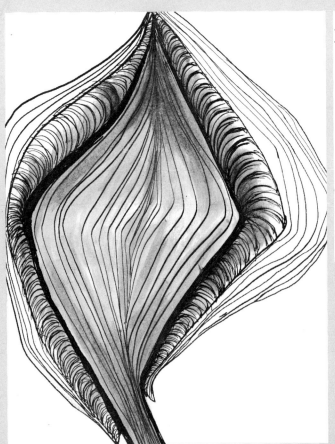

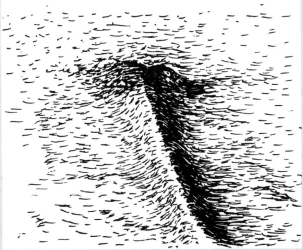

FIG. 11-11

FIG. 11-12

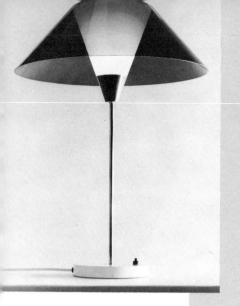

FIG. 11-13

FIG. 11-14

FIG. 11-15

FIG. 11-13

TABLE STUDY LAMP
John Hildred, designer
(General Electric Company,
Ltd. Photograph by Council
of Industrial Design, London)

FIG. 11-14

*Pressures in nature: the
vertical tree prevents the
great boulder from falling.
Opposing forces create a
momentary equilibrium. The
forms and spaces have a
Cézanne-like simplification
and integration (see Chapter
12, Form and Space).*

FIG. 11-15

ABSTRACT IN BLACK, WHITE,
BROWN, AND OLIVE (1960)
Victor Pasmore
*Forces are at work here. The
breakaway of the central
form from the mass on the
right has caused its movement to the left, where it is
exerting considerable force.*
(Victor Pasmore)

FIG. 11-16

LINEAR MOTIF (1961)
Victor Pasmore
*A dynamic composition of
energized hairlines. One has
the feeling that in five
minutes time the whole arrangement will have changed
completely.*
(Victor Pasmore)

FIG. 11-17

ABSTRACT IN BLACK AND
WHITE (1960)
Victor Pasmore
*A study of the disturbance of
space by forces. The lines of
force seem to extend, while
the pressure masses expand
inexorably to fill the space.*
(Victor Pasmore)

FIG. 11-18

THE CREATION OF ADAM
(1508-1512)
Michelangelo
(Sistine Chapel, Rome.
Photograph by Anderson)

FIG. 11-16

FIG. 11-17

FIG. 11-18

141

as we now know, spatial regularity and directional uniformity can reduce it to a minimum (Figs. 11-15 to 11-17). Possibly the greatest painting in which tremendous forces are held for a moment in a state of equilibrium is Michelangelo's "Creation of Adam," on the ceiling of the Sistine Chapel in Rome (Fig. 11-18).

In this great design, the forces producing the parallel movements of God and Adam are, for a fraction of time, held suspended, as the point thrusts of their outstretched arms and extended forefingers create an intense, yet delicate, stability— a stability charged with electrical energy. The visual dynamics in this painting are strongly buttressed by its deeply significant religious content.

We should now be able to recognize the dynamic elements in architecture (Fig. 11-19), in painting and sculpture (Fig. 11-20), in industrial design, and in nature (Fig. 11-21). Your drawings of forces in this series of experiments are actually symbols of force. Such symbols derived from personal experience and knowledge of the forces affecting form and disturbing space, can be one approach to abstract art. And the designer of artifacts should be aware of the pressures and forces symbolized by the line systems we have described and used.

The essence of composition in art is the disposition of forms in space, and that is what we have been dealing with in this section. We have been concerned with the movement tendencies between forms produced by the play of forces responsible for their present position in space. We have also studied the pressure forces operating between the parts of a single object. Attempting to understand composition without an awareness of the dynamic relationships that exist between forms in space, or between the several parts of one form, is like trying to speak French without knowing a word of the language.

In the plates accompanying this section, the three designs by Victor Pasmore, a contemporary English artist, illustrate particularly well what we have said here. Although they are abstract art, they reveal the forces that govern the disposition of things in the world of space.

FIG. 11-19

STAIRWAY, OFFICES IN LONDON
(1958)
Erno Goldfinger, architect
An example of the centripetal force in architecture. The spiral movement through space is initiated and sustained by forces originating at the center.
(The Architectural Review, London)

FIG. 11-20

ESCAPE AND OPPRESSION
Ernest Mundt
The massive concentration of power in the downward moving point thrust effectively contains the more dispersed thrust force that is attempting to move up and out.
(Ernest Mundt. Associated Press News Photograph)

FIG. 11-21

Pressures in nature: rocks in a state of equilibrium. But move one of the rocks and gravitational force would cause the structure to collapse, as each rock would move to a new position until it met an opposing pressure force. The pressures which are producing the stability of this structure can be visually experienced; there is no need to place a finger between the stones.
(Photograph by Wayne Bitterman)

FIG. 11-20

FIG. 11-19

FIG. 11-21

12

the
equilibrium
of forces in landscape

FIG. 12-1

THE THEBAID
Gherardo Starnina (?)
(*Uffizi Gallery, Florence*)

In this final chapter of Part One, form and space must be brought together and must be seen in a closer association. The two preceding chapters have already started us in this direction. An introduction was made in Form V to the structural organization of surface and the dynamic aspect of form. This was followed in Space IV by an examination of how the dynamic factor operates in space between objects and between the parts of a single object. We must now take the dynamic aspects of both form and space out of the studio and into the spacious world of landscape. By so doing, we shall see how integral are the relationships between them.

Like a leitmotiv, running through this whole book is one constant message—that art is concerned with clarifying particular aspects of our world, aspects perceived through those intellectual and intuitive processes that trigger the act of drawing. Artists such as Perugino, Leonardo, Cézanne, and Matisse have been mentioned in earlier chapters, always to reinforce this message. Now, in this the most difficult section of the book, the inspiration will come almost entirely from Paul Cézanne, the French painter who was born in 1839 and died in 1906. We shall analyze the dynamics of landscape; and in concentrating on this, we shall complete our discussion of forces, begun in the two previous chapters. Form and space

145

will now be brought together, and we shall become aware of the pressure each bears on the other. These patterns of reciprocal pressures between form and space, as seen in Cézanne's landscape paintings, reveal a universe of energy and matter held in a state of dynamic stability.

First, *how* do we perceive space? If you think about this, you will realize that an awareness of space occurs only because we are aware of form. If there were no form to touch or to see as substantial shape, then how would we be aware of nothingness, or nonshape . . . or space? So we really start off by thinking of form as *nonspace* and of space as *nonform*. Make sure you understand this concept before reading on. Figure 11-1 provides a helpful illustration. In the three drawings, groupings of black marks are separated by varying regions of space. The more these marks converge, the more the space is compressed. If the marks come completely together, they lose their individual identity and merge into a conglomerate form. Where there was space, there is now form. In such a merging of these marks—a movement of the marks—a force must act on the marks and *against* space. And when this new conglomerate form is complete, it continues to exist because it continues to exert a force or pressure against space. Were it not to do so, the form would disintegrate, because space, pushing back against it, would meet no resistance. This system of reciprocal pressures between form and space is explained by Newton's Third Law which states, "That for every action there is an equal and opposite reaction." Thus we have a pattern of pressure systems, of forces compressing space to produce form, of form continuing to exert pressure on space to counteract the equal and opposite reacting pressure space exerts on it—in short, an interplay of pressures between space and form. It is by such an interplay of pressures that the jet aircraft gains its momentum. The burning gases forced out at the rear of the jet exert tremendous pressure on space; it is the reacting thrust of space to this pressure which rams the aircraft forward. This reacting pressure is the *force* which moves the aircraft in space.

Space can now be visualized as a region identified as space by virtue of the "marker buoys" of form present in it. We know form as an occupant of space, exerting pressure against space and, in its turn, invoking a reacting pressure of space

146

against it. Thus, these reciprocal pressure patterns are in operation *once form is introduced into a region*. Through these pressures, form exists and is allowed to continue its existence; for were this pressure system to cease operating, then there would presumably be a disintegration of form, and also of space, since without form we do not know space.

Now we can get a better idea of why form and space are so closely related. No doubt you have heard of the word "claustrophobia," a morbid fear of being in closed rooms or narrow spaces. One often gets this feeling in a room overfull of furniture and drapery. Claustrophobia is a human reaction to strong pressure patterns operating in a restricted region; one longs to flee to a larger space. As forms continue to be introduced into a region, the pressures that build up between form and space become more and more complex. We ordinarily call this "overcrowding." But in a spatial context, it is a concentration of pressure that produces the tensions.

In a landscape, in the countryside, the pressure relationships between form and space are quite complicated. The space we call "the sky" envelops the moving growing forms of nature (and where there is a growing movement, there is an intensification of pressure) and hovers over the pressure swell of the earth, the skyward thrust of mountains and the gravity pulled rocks. The artist has long been sensitive to these complex pressure patterns; even in the fourteenth century they were expressed in art.

In the painting, "The Thebaid" (Fig. 12-1) by the fourteenth-century Florentine painter, Starnina, the thrusts of the earth against space are powerfully felt. The small trees standing against the sky seem subject to the most intolerable pressures from space (gravity is not very strong); they almost collapse as one looks at the picture. Newton's Third Law is in some danger here!

The importance of Paul Cézanne as a landscape artist lies in his introduction of space-form pressure patterns in art. For Cézanne, space was nonform and form was nonspace. Before Cézanne, artists had sensed these pressure forces; since Cézanne, they have been consciously aware of them. Look for a moment at this drawing "Valley with a Bright Cloud" (Fig. 12-2) by the English artist, Samuel Palmer (1805-1881).

This is a drawing weighty with pressures. Every leaf, every

147

blade of grass is growing against the opposition of space. Every form reveals the hidden pressure of its own swell or point thrust. The drawing is alive with point thrusts, centripetal thrusts, and pressure thrusts, although Samuel Palmer was undoubtedly not thinking in such terms when he made the drawing. But notice how the forms are in opposition: the log is pushing against the ground, and the ground against the log; the trees and bushes push against the sky, and the sky pushes back against them. The drawing is so "pressurized" that you feel the intrusion of one more form would cause an explosion. If one more toadstool were to break through the ground, the scene would blow up.

Now we must turn to Cézanne to see Newton's Third Law in operation, to see the pressures between form and space brought together into what could be a contradiction of terms —dynamic stability. Although this reproduction of "Mont St. Victoire" (Fig. 12-3) is in black and white, it will serve our purpose in discussing Cézanne's pressure patterns.

Compare this painting with the Palmer drawing. In the Cézanne, one is not aware of the opposition between form and space, as one is when regarding the Palmer. There is no opposition between form and space in Cézanne; in almost all of his painting he manages to achieve a stability, a harmony of pressures which convey a feeling of permanence. It is, in fact, difficult to distinguish between form and space in a Cézanne landscape, so closely are they integrated. How does he do it? It is achieved by his developing a structural design for his picture which both reveals and stabilizes the hidden pressures of form and space. In this pictorial design, Cézanne simplifies the natural form to a shape which suggests the pressure force of the form. Similarly, space is not treated as mere emptiness, but it becomes a shape suggesting the pressure force of that particular region as it opposes forms in the vicinity (Fig. 12-4). The painting that results is a visual statement of Newton's Third Law. It is Cézanne's way of creating a visible order in landscape; he reveals the invisible reality of pressure forces which lie behind the phenomena of form and space, the reality of *how* the world is, as explained by physical science.

As we study the "Mont St. Victoire," it is the stillness, the sense of permanence that strikes us. With all the pressure tensions that are revealed, it is Cézanne's genius to hold them

FIG. 12-2
VALLEY WITH A BRIGHT CLOUD
Samuel Palmer
(By courtesy of the Ashmolean Museum, Oxford)

FIG. 12-3
MONT SAINTE-VICTOIRE SEEN
FROM BIBEMUS QUARRY
(c. 1898-1900)
Paul Cézanne
(The Cone Collection, The Baltimore Museum of Art)

FIG. 12-2

FIG. 12-3

in a state of equilibrium. By permanence, then, we mean nondisintegration. Equilibrium or permanence represent pressures under control, and Cézanne was a master at exercising this control in his landscapes. The exercises in this chapter are concerned with the rather difficult concepts that have been presented here.

THE EXPERIMENTS

We are to make three drawings of landscape. Select some small and intimate corner of a landscape which has positive character and distinct features with which one can come to grips, rather than a widespreading vista.

The first drawing is straightforward. Using pen, pencil, charcoal, or brush—any drawing medium—draw just what you see with as much expression as you can. The sketch should be about 12″ x 9″ in size (Fig. 12-5). When it is finished, keep it easily accessible, for you will be working from it for the other two drawings.

The second drawing is to be of the same landscape; but this time, rather than concentrating on the immediate appearance of the view, try to reduce the forms in the landscape to a shape which suggests their pressure against space. The drawing will be one of suggested pressure forces of forms. It is better to start by working outdoors, to see, feel and intuitively grasp for yourself the pressure of the landscape forms against space. Do this by making many small drawings of forms or parts of forms. In these drawings, try to reduce the form to a shape which suggests how and where it exerts its dominant thrust against space. This will vary between the extremes of a point thrust, and a swelling pressure thrust spread over an area. Centripetal thrusts will not be so common, as this force operates more usually in space (air currents) than in form. But we will not attempt a similar reduction of *space* to pressure-shaped regions in this experiment, although this could be a further development of a fourth and more complex drawing.

To be sure we understand what is meant by the "pressure-force" shape of form, let us examine it in more detail.

FIG. 12-4

Sketch extracts from the paintings of Paul Cézanne indicate the pressure shapes given to form and space in landscape.

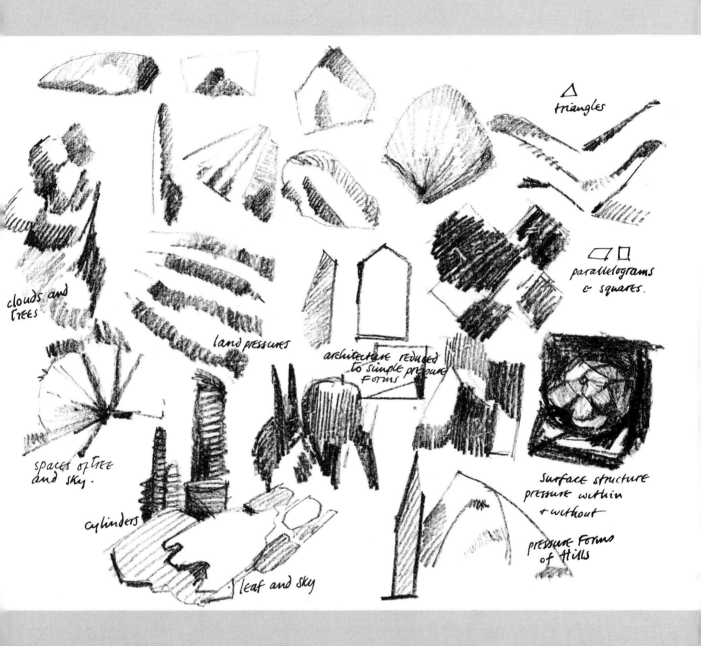

triangles

parallelograms & squares.

clouds and trees

land pressures

architecture reduced to simple pressure forms

surface structure pressure within + without

pressure forms of hills

spaces of tree and sky.

cylinders

leaf and sky

Pressure-force shape

You will remember that in the preceding chapter, Space IV, lines of force were used to represent the forces operating between objects. These lines suggested the directions of the forces that had brought the objects to their present position or the pressure forces between the parts of a single object. In this experiment, we are not concerned with *movement,* but with the thrust against space exerted by an object from one position, the position in which we perceive the object. Consequently, we need not a line of force, but an area of force, or what we might call a "pressure-force shape." It must have area, mass or volume, and reveal whether the surface is plane or curved, regular or irregular. Obviously, there will be suggestions in such a figure of point thrusts or swelling pressure thrusts, but they must be a part of, and subordinate to, the whole figure. The pressure-force shape is an abstraction from the natural form, to symbolize how, and in which direction, the form exerts its dominant thrusts into and against space. The sketches in Fig. 12-4 show how Cézanne simplified form, and gave shape to space, to reveal their pressure relationships, in a structural design that looks like interlocking pieces of a jig-saw puzzle.

Figure 12-6 shows some examples of forms reduced to simple pressure-force shapes, although these are crude and obviously contrived by comparison with Cézanne's forms.

You should now be reasonably familiar with your landscape subject, having made one complete drawing and several small ones of it. With these drawings before you, redraw the landscape, again about 12" x 9", and simplify all the forms to pressure-force shapes. If you bear in mind what has been said about pressure shape, you can probably assess the pressure aspect of an object instinctively. Also, sensitivity to the tactile qualities of the forms can prompt the hand to "feel" the pressures, and be aware of them in this way. And finally, you may become aware of the pressure implications of forms through a mental appreciation of the laws of physical science. In all three ways, some imagination is required.

Figure 12-7 provides a good illustration of the simplification of landscape forms to pressure-force shapes, producing what might be called a "pressure abstract" drawing. Figure 12-7

FIG. 12-5

Direct landscape drawing.

is not a complete drawing. It is but a step on the way to a more integrated abstract design where the space regions surrounding the forms would also be given a pressure-force shape, in order to reveal the reciprocal pressures exerted on form by space. But significantly, in this drawing form has been reduced to abstract shapes, symbolic and expressive of pressures felt, rather than seen.

We come now to the third and final drawing. If the previous drawing can be called a "pressure abstract" drawing, then this one can be described as a "force movement" abstraction. Our concern will be with the dynamic relationships existing in space between all the forms in the region. In a study of the first drawing, Fig. 12-8, we shall examine the inclining relationship of objects, either toward each other, away from each other, grounded by gravitational pull, or moving up into the sky, and try to discover what type of force brought the objects to their present position. The three types of force we have previously described in Space IV are:

1. The point thrust moving in a straight line; think of the vertical growth of a tree or plant, or the downward pull of gravity.

2. The centripetal thrust uncoiling itself from a central impetus like a spring; think of currents in air or water.

3. The pressure thrust of force distributed over a large surface area; think of the wind, of tide water, of the scooping force of glacier movement, or the swelling growth of a watermelon.

We have demonstrated how forces operate in the preceding chapter; the water pushing the stones of the river bed, gravity forces rolling rocks down hillsides, the growth forces of nature pushing up trees, and the equilibrium gained in architecture when forces are deliberately countered and the fall of a roof or a wall is thus prevented. We should associate force with the idea of movement. But although a pressure is a force, it suggests a more static state of affairs. It suggests an opposition to movement. When you blow up a balloon, you oppose the air pressure; when you place a book on a table, you oppose the pull of gravity; in both cases, you have the action of a force against an opposing force. Consequently, the movement is comparatively limited, or you have a stationary situation. Here lies

FIG. 12-6

Form reduced to simple figures representing pressure force against space.

FIG. 12-7

Forms from the direct landscape simplified to pressure-force shapes. A pressure-abstract drawing.

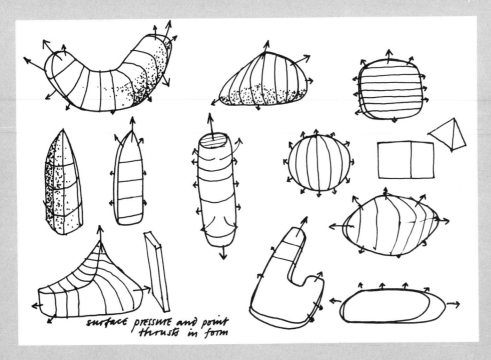

surface pressure and point
thrusts in form

FIG. 12-6

FIG. 12-7

the difference between the "pressure abstract" drawing and the "force movement" one to be produced in the third drawing. Look at your first landscape drawing again. What are the dynamic factors involved? What forces have disposed these forms? You will be able to distinguish between *growth* forces, *gravity* forces, or *elemental* forces (wind, water). Each of these may operate via the point thrust, the centripetal thrust, or the pressure thrust.

Using the linear symbols for these forces, make a "force movement" drawing expressing the dynamic factors responsible for the disposition of forms of your first landscape drawing. This will mean creating a spatial design representing the forces that have acted, and are still acting, on the forms in the landscape. The point thrust symbol could represent the growth force of a tree or a blade of grass. The forms themselves need not appear in such a drawing.

Figure 12-9 is a "force movement" abstraction that has been made from the parent drawing, where signs and symbols have replaced objects.

Conclusions

In this section we have attempted to combine two concepts: that of strong forces that produce *movement* and of forces in opposition that produce *pressure*. Both play an important part in the dynamics of art and design. Since this is a long and involved section of complex propositions, we will try to sum up the most important ideas behind these drawing experiments.

1. *The derivation of the abstract form*

As the artist probes beyond the appearance of things, other aspects of reality impinge on his awareness. In this study of space and form, we have been concerned with the invisible rather than the visible. In so doing, we have used signs and symbols which attempt to describe the forces that lie behind the world of appearances. Form is thus reduced to a symbol, and space is rendered meaningful by signs. The result is an abstract or nonrepresentational design. It is important to realize that these new abstract forms now constitute powerful visual images in their own right; they can even be used and developed without further recourse to the object. The artist

FIG. 12-8

Direct landscape drawing.

today realizes that he is free to invent, from his own imaginative resources, new shapes of symbolic and emotive power, and the object is no longer the first stimulus. Unfortunately, too many people consider themselves to be working in "the abstract" when all they are doing is producing jazzy patterns or derivative clichés. That is why these experiments are important. They provide a clue to how art works, how it is rooted in a tradition of inquiry, and they show that "modern art" has not just dropped from the sky. Cézanne blazed a trail to a new visual revelation and illustrated once again how necessary it is for the artist to have an inquiring eye and the capacity for imagination. It is the eye that triggers the intuition, the intellect, or the feeling, whichever happens to be the dominant muse for the artist.

2. *Forces of pressure*

The relationship of form to space, and space to form, can be perceived as a system of reciprocal pressure patterns. These patterns provide one ingredient of the dynamic in art and are the basis of the work for the second landscape drawing. Once again, this is an aspect of the invisible reality behind the scenes. Note the closely integrated structure of form with space—a synthesis of form and space—in this "Still Life" by the English painter, Ben Nicholson (Fig. 12-10). The forms are simplified to shapes that suggest their pressure potential, while the immediate space is organized into defined regions which exert pressure against the forms. At the same time, giving space a positive shape in this way helps us to appraise the aesthetic quality of the forms themselves. In still life as in landscape, space and form are complementary to each other.

3. *Forces of movement*

Forces of movement provide a second ingredient of the dynamic in art and govern the compositional elements in design. Such forces have been described at length in Space IV and in the discussion of the third landscape drawing in this chapter. As we perceive the positions of the forms in the landscape before us, we realize that their arrangement is due to the action of forces. Look at the elegant drawing by Victor Pasmore reproduced in Fig. 12-11. In it, the forces moving through space—point thrust, pressure thrust or centripetal—have created

FIG. 12-9

The direct landscape reduced to signs and symbols representing the force movements involved in the landscape. A force-movement abstraction.

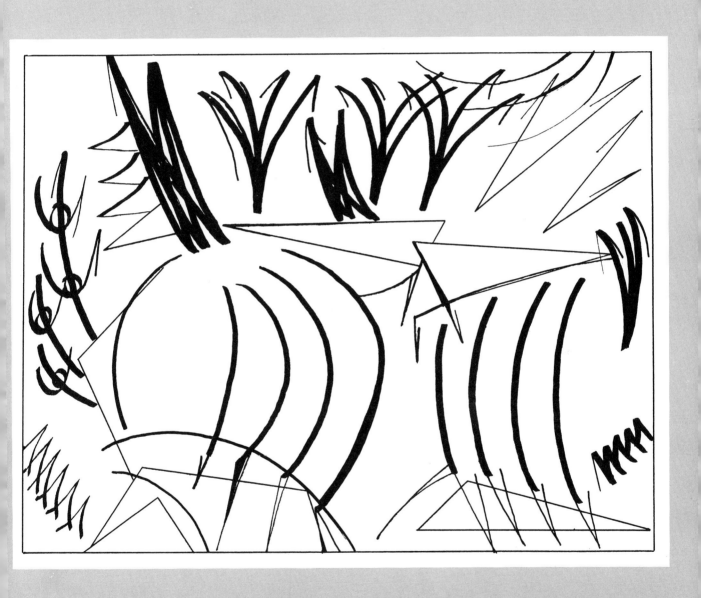

compartments, or defined regions of space. Notice the movement *between* these compartments. The space immediately inside the frame becomes part of the space of the inner rectangle, via the thrust of the heavy black line. No region can escape the forces at work. Even space outside the frame is part of the picture. One can imagine how objects within these regions would be affected by these forces, although the objects themselves do not appear in the drawing. The artist, in this drawing, sharpens our awareness of space by revealing to us the forces, rather than the forms.

4. *Possibilities of development*

The drawings you made should open the door to an invisible world of forces, forces of movement and of pressure. They are really shorthand notes that may be developed into paintings or used for ideas in design and research problems. They are also one introduction to abstract art. These drawings could become as meaningful as those of Pasmore and Nicholson, but only if you develop a spirit of inquiry, a heightened awareness of the possible causes of physical phenomena, and an imaginative ability to express your attitude and your understanding through drawing.

FIG. 12-10

STILL LIFE (1931-1936)
Ben Nicholson
(*Collection the British
Council*)

FIG. 12-11

LINEAR MOTIF (1961)
Victor Pasmore
(*Victor Pasmore*)

FIG. 12-10

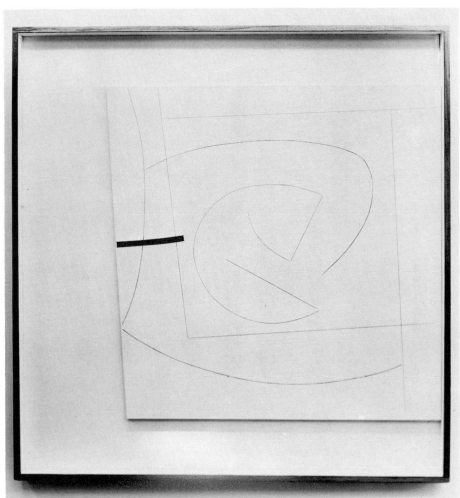

FIG. 12-11

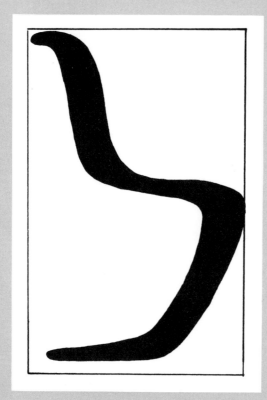

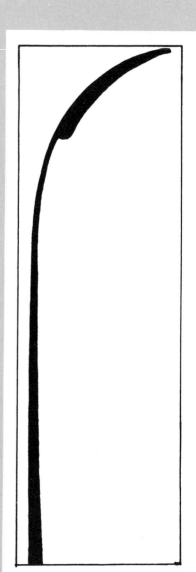

REVIEW

Form I

An awareness of skeletal form, an ability to express it in drawing, a realization of how summarily its limbs divide space, and a knowledge of when to use linear structure in drawing and design problems—all should be developed through further work. The drawing experiments suggested below provide opportunities for development.

1. Consciously apply the skeletal structure of natural objects to the designing of screens, street lamps, wood and metal chair frames, or similar artifacts (see Review Figures 1 and 2).

2. By means of articulated skeletal structures, experiment with the figure in action and repose, with or without the model.

3. From observation of forms that are strongly skeletal and demand an appreciation and expression of linear structure, make still-life and plant drawings.

4. Draw imaginatively from the stimulation of trees, plants, biological magnifications of organisms, and other natural objects whose skeletal form encourages linear abstraction and personal expression.

5. Draw to give ideas for pictorial development; take your first inspiration from a linear organization of surface derived from some visual skeletal stimulus such as the tracery of floating pond weed, veins on the back of the hand, a bare vine in winter.

REVIEW FIG. 1

Drawings for a laminated wood chair frame, a concrete street lamp, and a metal screen. These drawings represent a development of the skeletal structure drawings made from natural objects. They reveal the student's increased awareness of space-to-form relationships in this type of object and his attempts to produce a linear form which possesses a strongly organic structure.

Drawing Marks I

A sensitivity to the quality of lines and marks, to degrees of tone, and to surface can be developed only by constant exposure to these aspects of drawing. Consequently, from time to time, further experiments must be suggested to call on the student's initiative in the selection of material and in the personal use he can make of them in both objective and non-objective experimental drawing.

Space I

Further work to continue the development of natural depth perception and spatial relationships can be accomplished in many different ways, but here are a few suggestions.

1. Reproduce a complex grid taken from one of the linear structure drawings of Form I (Chapter 1) and fill in a minimum of six spatial regions with freehand vertical lines. Create six positions in depth by varying the concentration of lines in each space and by changing line weight and quality. The same exercise can be repeated by filling in the grid spaces with paint, moving from black to gray to lighter gray, etc., according to the depth position desired.

2. Make a free charcoal drawing in a nonobjective composition that, once again, achieves spatial relationships through degrees of drawing weight and intensity of tone.

3. Achieve variations on the "space-grid" idea (see Fig. 10-3), in which surface textures create degrees of frontality or recession, through the use of collage materials, as in Review Figure 3.

4. Take a newspaper sheet containing type and photographs and allow your natural depth perception to operate over the areas of blackness, grayness, or comparative whiteness. Build up a grid with brush and line around these perceived areas of varying depth, allowing the grid line, by means of weight and quality, to emphasize and accentuate the depth positions of the perceived regions.

Form II

The many uses of the contour line as a means of expressing both space and mass volume are fairly obvious but further

REVIEW FIG. 2

A sheet of quick notes experimenting with a chair's skeletal structure and frontal and receding stripes, preparatory to producing finished drawings.

projects requiring the contour line are suggested as follows:

1. Draw the figure, from the model if possible, in many positions, as a series of contour volumes, perhaps *over* an articulated skeleton, as suggested in the review to Form I.

2. Try an expressive drawing of objects possessing strong mass form and/or holes, where both contour line and contour tone can realize the form. Experimenting with the dry brush and the finger as drawing instruments for both contour line and tone gives surprising results.

3. Draw free, imagined forms expressed through contour line and tone—forms in significant juxtaposition possessing pictorial suggestions.

4. Make free and imaginative drawings of space—of air formations, of smoke, vapor, steam, etc.—where form is moving and constantly changing.

5. Make large charcoal drawings (5' x 3') of imagined wood forms, using the contour line to produce a sweeping rhythm of arm movement (Fig. 4-16).

Form III

Perhaps it is not a good thing to develop too strong a conscious attitude to the aesthetic implications of form, as so much of this is intuitively present in a personal drawing. In any case, that which constitutes the aesthetic cannot be rigidly or even simply defined; but some awareness of it is helpful, and so the following suggestions for further development of this chapter are made.

1. Select a flower or a leaf which has a strong aesthetic appeal as form. Draw it freely, deliberately exaggerating the particular aspect that appeals. Observe the drawing and decide if it appeals as much as the original object. Analyze why the answer is "yes" or "no." Determine why, and when, over-idealization defeats its own ends.

2. To induce a mental and deliberate appreciation of form, take a simple cube, like the building brick, and draw it very lightly and quite large. Now work over this drawing by cutting into the cubic form and adding facets and more cubic volumes to produce a drawing of a sculptured brick form. Organize the design consciously and appraise

REVIEW FIG. 3

Black and white collage using type and newsprint. Notice the disposition of the heavier type to produce rhythms of dominance and to give focal emphasis to regions of space.

This is a development experiment to follow the intuitive brush-dabbing exercise.

it at each stage. Justify the design on intellectual grounds of proportion, symmetry, balance, etc.

3. Repeat the second exercise, this time freely and as the spirit moves you, with very little deliberation about the way you modify the brick cube. Compare the result with the first drawing and determine whether the deliberate or the free attitude has produced the more satisfactory design.

Space II

The instinctive tendency to organize space into "regions of space" by the introduction of form has been shown in this chapter. Further work in space perception and in the "designing" of space is best carried out as suggested for Space I.

Space III

Many experiments can be devised to attack the problem of consciously having to express space perception through drawing. Here are three suggestions.

1. Observe the operation of a water sprinkler on the grass in summer as it moves through a complete circle. Make a series of freehand sketches which indicate the height and curvature of the water jet's arc in perhaps fifteen or twenty positions throughout the complete circle of movement. In the studio, translate these sketches into one diagrammatic drawing which attempts to show the full circle of movement followed by the sprinkler, the constant or varying arcs of the jet in different positions on this circle, and the regions of space in depth created by the moving arc.

2. Using a series of lines of differing weight and quality, design a space-grid in which some areas are almost entirely enclosed by lines and therefore project forward, while others, more open, recede at various depths. Separately, design a simple form which suggests a fast-revolving, metallic body, and then draw this in four or five of the space regions. In the space which is most frontal, this body should be large and strong in line and weight; in the chosen space most receding, the revolving body should be small and light in drawing. In between

these two extremes, the size and weight of the body should depend upon the relative space position of the region it is to occupy. The drawing, when complete, should suggest a space region of infinite depth with materializing bodies flying in from outer space.

3. "Draw" with different types of wire, using a line in the air to work out various problems three-dimensionally; for example, "The Disappearing Square," "The Square and the Round," "Space Compressed," "Diminution of a Theme," and so on.

Form IV

The understanding and use of the structural unit is important principally to the designer. Some further experiments are as follows:

1. Build a free-standing model, using one repeating unit of structure; for example, matchsticks, plastic hair curlers, nails, paper clips, etc.

2. Make further imaginative drawings of "freaks" in nature, using an actual unit of structure taken from a natural object.

3. Design an architectural unit from which to construct a screen wall.

4. Examine some models of molecular structure—zinc or hemoglobin, for example. Select one that is not too complex and draw it simply as a system of lines and black blobs. Taking this drawing as the unit, create a complex pattern in a 9-inch square. At the same time, vary the line weight as the unit is repeated over the whole area to produce regions of depth in the spaces thus formed.

Form V

All drawings of complex surfaces demand visual analysis of the organization of planes, curves, and angles, automatically making the artist aware of the pressure forces operating in and on the object. The following exercises are suggested to continue this pressure force aspect of form.

1. Draw the forms made on material other than paper after it is crumpled, bent, squeezed, or subjected to any

other mechanical action. Use silk, aluminum foil, plastic sheeting, clay, etc., and notice the diverse surface formations created, owing to the different resistances of the various materials.

2. Draw still life made up entirely of complex, folded materials, from pleated paper to folded textiles.

3. Using a magnifying glass, make an enlarged drawing of wrinkled skin. There are several regions on the back of the hand and fingers that serve for this. Notice what happens to the surface when the skin is tensed by clenching the hand and when it is relaxed.

4. Make five drawings which illustrate the development of a form to complexity. First make a simple, solid triangle from a sheet of aluminum foil, and then push into it once, with a finger. Draw the result. Push in the triangle again at another point and draw the result. Proceed in this manner until five drawings have been produced.

5. Fill a drawing notebook with sketches of quarry walls, rock formations, rock surfaces, the wrinkles of cabbages and bark—anything, in fact, of interesting surface structure.

Form V: Surface texture

Some suggestions for further work to develop sensitivity to surface texture.

1. Ink over surfaces possessing interesting qualities and take a print on sensitive paper; for example, take a print from the end of a cut log. Build up a collection of such prints for reference purposes.

2. Experiment with the monoprint to produce textures. Select several differing surfaces from the prints and put them together in the form of a collage.

3. Select a poem that evokes mood, one that suggests laughter, sorrow, tranquillity, anger, and so on. Attempt to make a translation of the poem in terms of textures, either by collage, or drawing, or both.

Space IV

Many possible developments for this chapter are available in the drawings already made. These abstract sketches can be developed into full-scale abstract designs, incorporating tone, line, texture, and spatial depth, all of which have been previously discussed. Other suggestions would be

1. Set up still-life groups which have a strong dynamic factor operating (a bottle right on the corner of the table, almost falling off, or objects supporting other objects rather tenuously). Translate such a group into a drawing of forces, both movement and pressure.

2. Attempt to work out some design problems, such as possibilities for a six-light chandelier or a large water fountain. For a beginning express only the forces involved, both movement and pressure. See what *shapes* that might develop into the actual object are suggested by these force drawings.

Form and space

Again, developments here can be made from the abstract and semi-abstract drawings already made, as suggested for Space IV, above. Here are some other possibilities.

1. Draw additional landscapes that reduce space as well as form to pressure shape, to produce an integrated space-form pictorial structure.

2. Thinking of the same space-form integration, and either the pressure-abstract drawing or the force-movement drawing, work with still life, the figure, or the portrait, treating the space around the object or head, between the legs and arms, as shape positively related to the object, head or figure. Or draw from architecture and town-scape with the same intention. (Study the paintings of Lyonel Feininger, for example.)

3. Trees, particularly, make fine subjects for translation to force-movement patterns, with integrated spatial pressure regions. (Piet Mondrian's tree abstractions would repay study in this regard.)

PART TWO

vision

One major theme runs through Part Two. It is that the creative imagination feeds on images, that image begets image for the artist, as idea begets idea for the writer.

The word "image" as we use it has two meanings. It may signify the mental image, *the picture formed in the mind's eye as the result of ideas produced by some stimulus to the imagination. Or it may signify the* concrete image, *the drawing, painting, or object which possesses the power to stimulate the imagination. The concrete image may also be the practical result of an act of the creative imagination. Both types of image owe their significance to the human capacity for imaginative experience. All kinds of things can stimulate the imagination to produce mental images; but in the eight experiments in the second half of this book, we shall assume that the stimulus that most affects the imagination of the artist is the visual stimulus, the stimulus of the thing seen and the thing experienced. Any visible thing may be such a stimulus; and when it is, it may accordingly be termed a "concrete image." The degree of imaginative significance we are capable of giving to things depends on how well-developed our vision is. We use "vision" here to mean the ability to recognize the potential aesthetic significance of the thing seen, its secretive meaning and associations, its power to heighten mood, or its possible emergence as a symbol.*

Not everybody possesses a capacity for the type of vision we are talking about here; yet many people, when faced with unusual objects or interesting drawings, will make some kind of imaginative jump to a new and more significant mental image. This is the process we called the "developing idea" in art. Each experiment in Part Two is concerned with these principles. They provide a concrete image of some kind to set off the reflex-like workings of the imagination. The mental image thus engendered is then produced in graphic form by drawing. This drawing is a new concrete image and inspires the imagination to a further picture in the mind, which is realized, in its turn, through drawing. And so the process goes on until the imagination has exhausted itself. The creative imagination in the visual arts works by these means. It is a truism to state that without vision there is no art.

173

13

the

monoprint

A monoprint is a print made from a design that is engraved in ink lying on a flat surface. Only one, or at the most two prints can be taken from such an inked surface. In Drawing Marks I (Chapter 2), a series of lines and marks was made by direct application of ink to paper, and each line or mark had its own quality, its own expressive character in terms of tranquillity or agitation, frontality or recession. If you draw lines on the inked surface of a piece of glass, as you did previously on a sheet of paper, these lines or marks can be translated to paper by taking a print from the glass plate. But these lines and printed marks will bear a different quality from those drawn on paper, for they make a stronger and more immediate visual impact; they possess a special dramatic quality. Assuming that the ink used is black ink, the dramatic quality is present because white lines on a black background are visually more forceful than black lines on white. It is this forceful quality of the monoprint drawing that we are to pursue.

We should explain what is meant by the "forceful quality" of a drawing. It appears when we recognize marks of drawing that are charged with a possibility for development, as opposed to drawings that kindle no such imaginative sparks. Such forceful drawings catch our attention immediately and continue to involve us imaginatively. The significant thing about the

Figure study by the author. This is a monoprint from the glass slab. It indicates the rapidity of drawing that this medium demands and the possible subtlety of line and tone obtainable from the inked glass plate.

175

monoprint method is that it heightens the visual impact of the drawing, and therefore allows us greater opportunity to recognize its imaginative significance and its potential development. To draw successfully on glass, over the slippery surface of ink, now with line, now wiping out areas of tone, demands spontaneity and intuition rather than deliberation and reason. The freedom this medium gives the artist enables him to produce a greater range of marks that are vital and instinctive and which also have a forceful quality. Artists and designers require a capacity for vision; one element of this, as we have seen, is an ability to recognize the potential aesthetic significance of the thing seen. Consequently, any medium which aids the recognition of this factor in the images created through drawing should be explored.

In the work described in Drawing Marks I, you discovered that all kinds of "instruments" can be used to make drawing marks. On the inked glass plate, an even greater variety can be used. The range in the kind of marks that can be made on the glass is almost unlimited; no other medium allows such rapid expression of a mood, an idea, or an attitude. Consequently, you should approach the monoprint freely and with a certain spirit of adventure. At the same time, you should remember the statements made about "line quality" in Drawing Marks I. But the monoprint introduces another factor, that of tone (the degrees of transition from light to dark), an important aspect of monoprint technique that will be described in company with line.

THE EXPERIMENTS

The equipment required is as follows: a sheet of glass about 18″ x 15″, some tubes of black water-color printing ink, a roller for inking the glass, an absorbent printing paper or newsprint paper.

Experiment 1

This is a line experiment. First squeeze out an inch or so of ink onto the center of the glass plate, and then roll it out evenly over the whole glass area. Roll it well in several counterdirections, so that the ink layer is evenly distributed and

FIG. 13-1

The monoprint: lines drawn in the ink with wood.

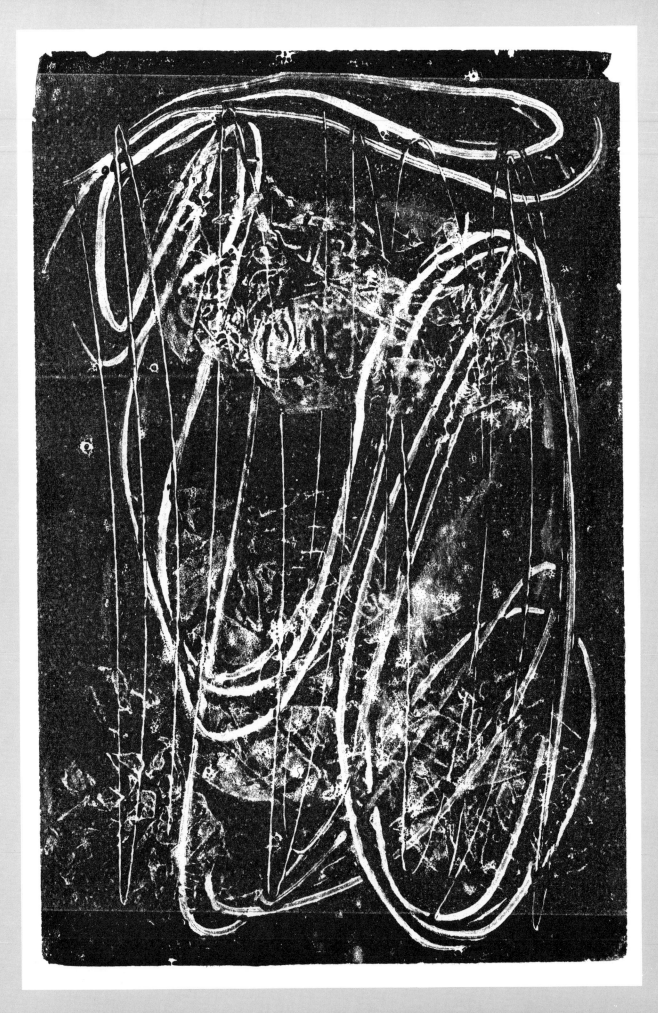

"tacky" to the roller. Now, take a piece of wood (a matchstick or small twig will do) and shape it to a flat, chisel end. This is the first instrument to use in drawing in the ink, and it should be used to produce a line of varying widths as the sharpened end is turned from the flat to the sharp edge as it moves over the glass. There is no conscious aim to this first line. Just work freely, moving the whole arm rather than only the wrist, and produce a rhythmic movement over the whole of the glass area. Stop whenever you feel you have disturbed the ink enough. If a sheet of printing paper is now placed over the plate, then rolled over with a clean roller (or firmly impressed by hand) and peeled off, you will see an interesting reproduction of the line drawn in the ink (Fig. 13-1). Close examination of this printed line will reveal that every subtle nuance of thick and thin, every break, and every variance in the pressure used to make it is faithfully reproduced. A dramatic element of intensity is added because the line is white surrounded by an area of black. But you will notice, too, that this background area is not uniformly black; some parts are grayer than others, or more grained and textured, while other areas are smooth and deep in their blackness. This variation in background is caused by the differing pressures of the roller and the directional changes made by the roller as the printing paper was impressed on the glass. This textural interest of the monoprint background helps give the drawing its forceful intensity.

Now try a drawing instrument of a quality quite different from that of a piece of wood. Roll out the ink smoothly over the glass once more and draw in it with your finger and fingernail, then try a piece of wire (Fig. 13-2), the edge of a folded piece of stiff paper, a piece of rubber, and, finally, press a length of string down into the ink. When you take the impressions from these various line markings, you will get a print of differing types of white line, forcefully presented. It is important to notice how these lines of the monoprint differ from black lines produced on paper by pen, pencil, or charcoal. Which do you think is the more dramatic and forceful?

Experiment 2

This second experiment is concerned with areas of tone rather than line, and with qualities of tone in gray areas between the extremes of black and white. For this work you will need

FIG. 13-2

The monoprint: lines drawn in the ink with wire.

FIG. 13-3

FIG. 13-3

*Areas of tone (with some line)
produced by drawing with a
hairbrush in the ink. The
print has strong pictorial
suggestions of animal forms.*

FIG. 13-4

*A result obtained by scraping
the ink in a free and rhythmic
manner with various folded,
stiff pieces of card.*

FIG. 13-4

two brushes (a hair and a bristle brush), some pieces of strongly textured rag or canvas, a sponge, wire wool—anything, in fact, possessing a textural surface that will disturb the surface of the ink; you can even use your fingers or the palm of your hand to impress the ink. Once again, prints should be taken at any interesting stage of development, or printing can be delayed until a complex superimposition of marks has been made on the glass. A good starting method is to use one or other of the brushes (you will notice later the different tonal regions produced by hair or bristle) to stroke the ink without consciously thinking in terms of a design.

Don't overcrowd the glass area with these brush markings, and take a print of them first before going on to use the other equipment you've assembled. This print will have black areas of background and gray areas of texture where the brush marked the ink. The surface will appear more subtly variegated than the prints obtained of lines made with the wooden stick, since it is composed of the more delicate markings of the brushes. There may be strong pictorial suggestions produced by the textured shapes these brushed areas of tone have un-intentionally created (see Fig. 13-3).

Now let's take this work a little further and see what happens when we scrape off some of the ink. With the glass freshly inked and using either a corner of a rag or the edge of a folded piece of paper, or even parts of your hand, remove large areas of ink from the glass and then work over the whole plate once more with the brush, wood, or finger, dragging the remaining inked areas into the wiped places. The result is a combination of blacks, whites, and grays, multi-textured and charged with a possibility for development (see Figs. 13-4 to 13-6).

Experiment 3

This final piece of work is even more experimental. Select one or two objects such as bottle tops, hair curlers, interesting pieces of wood, bamboo, rush matting, or a simple paper clip and impress them one at a time into the freshly inked plate. Figures 13-7 to 13-10 will help explain how these "instruments" have been used. Place the object in the ink and pull it slightly to one side, or roll it around in the ink producing a range of

FIG. 13-5

*A self-sufficient visual state-
ment made by drawing lines
in the ink and scraping off
the ink with folded card.*

FIG. 13-6

*The forms in this monoprint
were made solely by scraping
the plate with a piece of
rough card.*

FIG. 13-5

FIG. 13-6

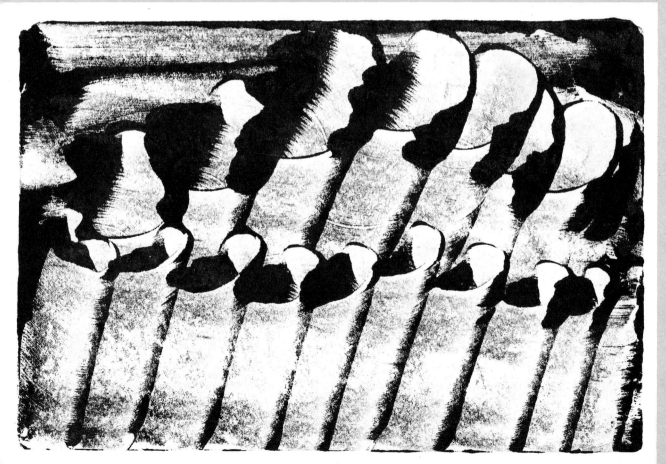

FIG. 13-7

FIG. 13-7

In this example a crumpled handkerchief was pressed into the ink. Notice the good positioning of the impression in the rectangle of black.

FIG. 13-8

Bottle tops were used here to produce these elliptical markings. The slight twist given to the instrument while in the ink gives the mark a three-dimensional quality and creates a sense of depth in the black space.

FIG. 13-9

A plastic hair curler and a short length of bamboo were used to make these distinctive marks in the ink.

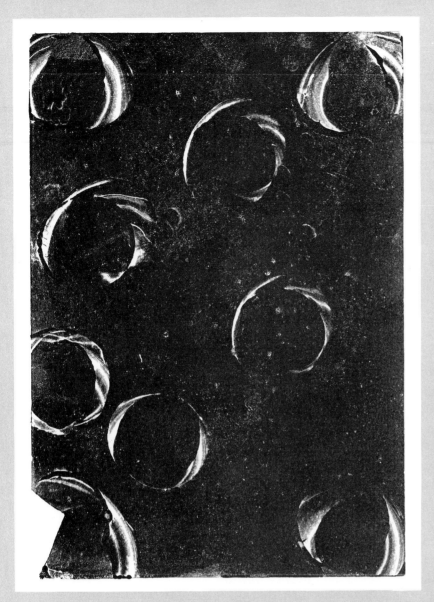

FIG. 13-8

FIG. 13-9

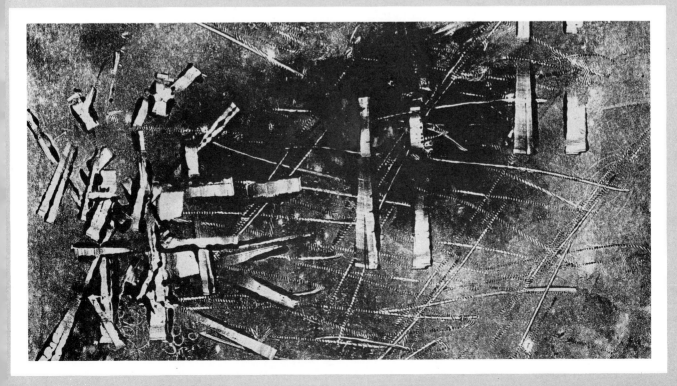

superimposed images. Disturb the ink as many times as seem necessary to produce an interesting image. The print, like its predecessors, is forceful and dramatic, and obviously the strange white forms could not occur on a normal drawing. They have come from a deliberate exploitation of monoprint characteristics. But they involve our imagination and stimulate our capacity for vision; we can see all kinds of pictorial and design possibilities in them—all kinds of shape—many regions of space. This is not to deny the prints significance as "drawings" in their own right; this significance will be touched on in the conclusion.

Conclusions

At the end of this series of experiments, you should have many prints from the glass plate, some interesting and some not so interesting, but all strong in terms of black and white. The images produced on each print owe their expressive quality to the character of the medium—to the sensitive printing surface of glass, to the fluid way water-color printing ink spreads on the glass, to the great variety of means that can be used to disturb the ink, and, finally, to the process of printing itself. But the medium, itself, cannot produce a work of art. To develop the artistic possibilities of the monoprint, to make prints that lead to new ideas about form and pictorial design, the artist must develop his ability to recognize the possible development of a drawing and extend his capacity for expression in the medium. The monoprint can help increase the artist's sensitivity to tone, line, and graphic image, but it is also a powerful medium in its own right. The sensitive artist who knowns the monoprint process well can produce fascinating prints by using the glass plate as a painter would use a canvas (Fig. 13-11). We have employed the medium here to extract images from the ink; later, in Vision VI (Chapter 19), we will use it as the painter might use it, and you will see there further evidence of its power and versatility as a serious drawing medium.

FIG. 13-10

These delicate markings in the ink were made by rolling a fir cone over the inked plate. The vertical lines were then drawn in with a wooden point.

FIG. 13-11

Figure study by the author.

FIG. 13-10

FIG. 13-11

14

addition and subtraction

Now that we have had an introduction to form, to space, and to drawing through line and tone, we should introduce the other basic element in art, the element of vision. Vision is the ability to respond imaginatively to the latent aesthetic power of an object or of a visual statement such as a sketch, a roughed-out design, or the first few brush strokes of a painting. Vision may be experienced at varying levels of intensity. At the highest level, the artist may be greatly moved as well as imaginatively transported. In this experiment, vision at a considerably lower level is called for—a capacity for personal involvement and decision in a design situation which is possessed by even the nonartist.

The creative process in the visual arts is usually triggered by some visual stimulus—something seen, however simple and tentative. From my own experience, and after talking to painters, architects, sculptors, and designers for many years, it becomes obvious that only rarely is a person able to visualize the whole or completed project in one flash of insight or inspiration. If most of us sit around waiting for such "inspiration" to strike, it is doubtful if we would ever produce anything. No, there is more to it than this. The theme for a work of art often grows out of a new and sudden awareness of some ordinary, perhaps familiar object, or of a few lines of an incom-

FIG. 14-1

THORN TREES (1946)
Graham Sutherland
A painting made after thorn bushes loomed terrible and significant to the eye and mind of the artist.
(Collection, British Council, London)

189

plete drawing. This new awareness of a thing seen we call "heightened perception," and heightened perception is the herald of vision. It was vision which resulted in the great series of thorn paintings produced a few years ago by the British painter Graham Sutherland (see Fig. 14-1).

A common thorn bush that the artist had passed by without notice on numerous walks, one day detached itself from its surroundings and loomed sharp and terrible to the eye and mind of the painter. For Sutherland, this was a moment of vision, and the spike of thorn later became the motif in paintings symbolizing the suffering and pain to which man is heir. It would be useless for any other artist to try to do the same thing without the vision of the inner meaning and significance residing in the thorns, for his painting would be merely a picture of a thorn bush. Even if we assume that this capacity for vision exists at an intense level for only a few great artists, we all have potentials for imaginative perception that we have not realized. To stretch our imaginations, it helps to build gradually, moving step by step from the first visual stimulus, each stage of development suggesting the next, until we can carry the theme no farther. The work described in this chapter is designed to encourage such chain-reaction growth of the imagination.

"I usually start by scratching about," a well-known industrial designer remarked in conversation one day. This is not a facetious statement. When he says "scratching about," he means that by making a series of scribbles, he will eventually see one that will suddenly leap out as the one with potential for development. But until he has something he can actually see, he has no base around which to build a theme.

There are, of course, endless ways to "scratch about." The least you need is a bit of paper—the back of an old envelope will do—and something to make a mark. The importance of this doodling process is that it produces images which in turn stimulate imaginative perception and, thus, new images in the mind. After many sheets are covered with what is apparently nothing of significance, they can be put aside, apparently wasted. If one returns to study them some minutes later, however, it is surprising how one shape, one partial form, one twist, one angle, one proportion, or one surface texture will suddenly stand out and suggest further development (Fig.

FIG. 14-2

DRAWING (1935)
Henry Moore
A drawing almost of the nature of a doodle, yet notice how the artist suddenly develops the forms suggested by the wandering line, as a twist or an angle helps an image to materialize.
(Collection, Edward Carter)

190

14-2). From this basic motif or design idea, a theme may be developed until it reaches a point of complete exploitation, when all further additions merely confuse the design. Then it is time to stop, before the intrinsic character of the theme is lost. But the ability to know when a drawing or a design is complete and total is one of the hardest for an artist to acquire.

The experiment described in this chapter attempts to follow the evolution of a design idea from its beginnings as a concrete image (the thing seen) to its proper conclusion. From a simple first mark, a cut on a linoleum block, we will move through a complex process of addition, until addition becomes subtraction (because eventually the block surface is reduced to an area beyond which additional cuts subtract from the printing surface). In the end, we return to a simple statement similar to our first mark, or rather to a negative of this first mark.

THE EXPERIMENT

The necessary equipment includes a block of linoleum about 5″ x 3″, one or two linoleum cutting tools, a glass slab, a roller, and a tube or so of black, water-color printing ink. The linoleum block can be used either horizontally or vertically, and the work may involve 15 to 25 operations. An operation consists of one or two cuts and the making of a print of the result.

To begin, make a cut anywhere on the virgin block of linoleum. It may be a simple, engraved line or the removal of a small area of the block; do not think long about it, just do it. Figure 14-3 illustrates the first stage.

When the first cut has been made, ink the block with the roller that has been moistened in the ink spread thinly over the glass, and take a print from the block on a sheet of newsprint. The result is not particularly significant. You will see a large rectangle of black broken only by a small white mark. It did not take a great deal of thought or cause you much worry to make the first cut because there was no "subject matter" to create a mental barrier. Now look again at this first print, for your next step is to make a second cut or series of cuts (two or three can be done together) which enlarge on, or develop, the first mark. If two or three cuts are made, make sure that you limit yourself to a comparatively simple extension of the first cut. At this point, you will find yourself weighing the possibilities quite logically. You will be aware of the dominance of the large area of black; you will notice the direction in which the first mark seems to move; you will assess the mark's angular or curvilinear character. You will probably instinctively feel where and how you should make the second cut or cuts.

After this second cutting operation, take another print from the block. Do this on the newsprint beneath the first, in order to make some visual comparisons. You will notice that this print is not so all-over black as the first. The white lines or areas have moved further into the black, breaking it down, and a white pattern is emerging. This method of working should now be repeated, stage by stage. After each additional cut or small group of cuts, a print should be taken. On the block itself, with each cutting stage, when more and more of the surface printing area is disappearing, a white pattern will gradually emerge. After a number of these cuttings and printing stages (which will differ according to each person's method of working), half-way stage will be reached when the area of black remaining approximately balances the area of white. From this point on, as you extend the white marks into the now rapidly diminishing black, you will be achieving a complete reversal of your first prints. Then you had a few white lines in a black area; now you are left with a few black marks in a white area. By the time you take your final print, this reversal is complete. One black mark will stand in a large area of white.

To study all the prints together, mount them individually, in the order of their printing, on a large sheet of paper. (Each print should be numbered as you make it.) Mount the prints in columns with number 1 in the top left-hand corner and then continue the sequence as indicated in Fig. 14-4.

Conclusions

With all the prints mounted, you will now see more easily how the developing process has occurred. From the first, perhaps tentative mark, the block develops an increasing complexity, progressing through the stage of balanced black with white, until it succumbs to the disintegrating cuts of the final stages. The *high point of development* exists when the pattern of lines and shapes and the black and white distribution are just right. Disintegration starts when this balance is disturbed by the addition of just *one more mark*. And yet it is important to remember that you were never consciously subtracting anything, but actually always adding marks.

Eight chapters of this book are devoted to what is called vision or "the developing idea," which is nowhere better illustrated than by this sheet of prints. Look at Figs. 14-5 and 14-6 for a moment and pick out the most complex print of each series. Would it be possible, do you think, to arrive at this particular print *immediately* through a flash of inspiration? It is conceivable, of course—some artists do see the whole thing in their head before starting to work—but it is rare. We know as we look at these two illustrations that the most interesting black-white arrangement on both sheets grew out of a logical and intuitive appraisal of a visual fact—the fact of the first freely cut mark. From making that first step it has been a challenge to break down the solid weight of the block's dominant empty black area. Out of this challenge the design has grown.

Note that in both Fig. 14-5 and Fig. 14-6, the character of the design was determined at a very early stage in the cutting process. It was determined by the third print in both cases. It is difficult to imagine either of these designs having developed other than in the form we see them here. There are no inconsistencies at any stage, yet both these students at the outset declared how hopeless they were "at art." Once past the halfway stage, they gained in confidence and interest, for now the problem was one of organic growth; the white had to grow and eliminate the black. During this exercise, one of the students referred back to one of his earlier drawings of twig structure, to see again how space penetrates linear form.

This, then, is how most designing starts. It grows out of a basic theme which is imaginatively exploited until it reaches a stage of total completeness. In the words of one student busily engaged in scratching about on this particular experiment, "You begin to plan ahead. . . ."

FIG. 14-3
The first cut in the block.

FIG. 14-4
Method of mounting prints.

FIG. 14-5
Mounted series of prints.

FIG. 14-6
Mounted series of prints.

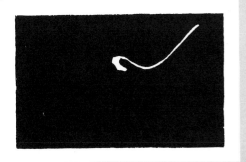

FIG. 14-3

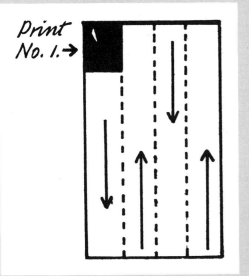

Print No. 1. →

FIG. 14-4

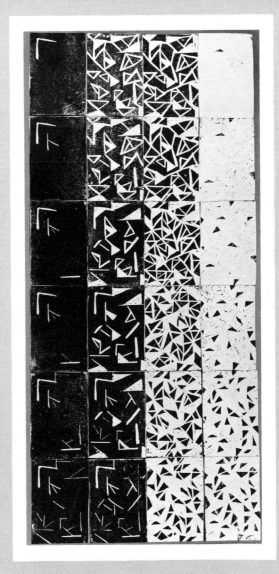

FIG. 14-5

FIG. 14-6

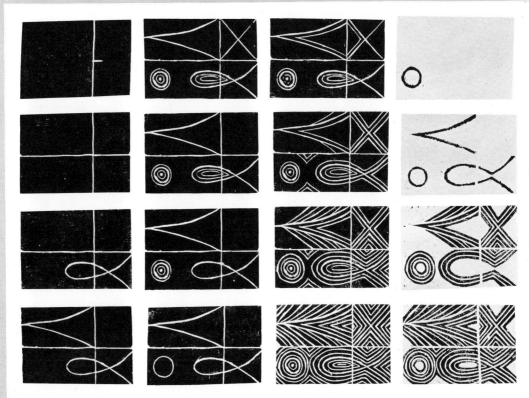

15

new shapes from old

The preceding work with the linoleum block demonstrated how we can build a simple theme into a full symphony of patterns. It enabled us to see when a process of development was complete. And we could also see when the development of the theme had not gone far enough, and when it had gone too far altogether.

Knowing when a work is complete, when any addition or subtraction can be only detrimental, is a major constituent of artistic ability. If you will look again at the drawing by Samuel Palmer (Fig. 12-2), you will perhaps feel that nothing more can be added without causing the taut pressure-patterns to break up. This drawing is thus complete.

Our next experiment is concerned with completeness. Like the exercise in Vision I (Chapter 14), it sets out to develop a theme, but this time in rather a different way, demanding a more conscious imaginative jump from the basic theme to the new shape. It also involves three-dimensional form rather than pattern.

The basic theme is bottle shape. The experiment is short and relatively simple, but it does reveal again that the ability to design results from a capacity to see beyond what *is*, to what *might be*. In the process of visualizing a new form for a familiar object, the artist will imaginatively assess both its structural

GLASSES
S. Fogelberg, designer
It is difficult to visualize any possible change in shape that would improve the form of these glasses. They have an ease of proportion and a purity of form that suggest completeness.
(Thomas Webb and Sons. Photograph by Council of Industrial Design, London)

197

and aesthetic refinement before embodying it through drawing as a concrete image.

THE EXPERIMENT

Ordinary glass bottles come in many varied shapes and proportions, some pleasing, some disturbingly ugly. The bottle,
like the snail's shell, is essentially an object of space volume,
a container whose space is enclosed, and consequently defined,
by a material substance. We have already discovered that the
continuously revolving contour line which moves in a continuous exploration of surface is an effective means of realizing
the structure of such objects of volume. But another quality
characterizes bottle shape: it is symmetrical or near-symmetri-
cal. Unlike the hole in the snail shell, a piece of wood, or a
cloud, the volume is symmetrical around an imaginary axis passing through the center of the bottle. When one draws a bottle,
then, it is helpful to draw this imaginary axis. As the bottle
swells and narrows around its axis, indicate on the axis, by
means of horizontal lines, the widest and the narrowest portions. This produces an imaginary skeletal structure like the
drawing note *a* in Fig. 15-1.

Here is an instance of skeletal form assisting in the drawing
of an object of volume, although it plays no real part in the
actual structure of the bottle.

Make a random selection of empty bottles, choosing four
or five different shapes. Set them up one at a time and make a
drawing of each, a drawing which attempts to explain the
structure of the bottle. Do several drawings on one sheet of
paper as in Fig. 15-1. Any haphazard grouping will do, for this
is not intended as a bottle composition. Use both the imaginary
skeletal axis and a combination of apparent outline and revolving contour lines to express the volume of each bottle.
Once you have "put the bottle together" in this way, it becomes
more significant as a structural form—you have looked inside as
well as out.

From this sheet of structural drawings, select two or three
which appeal to you most, and on a separate sheet of paper

redraw each bottle individually on a large scale, about 12 inches tall. Make these drawings in outline only. The very fact that the bottles have been drawn and understood structurally, as volume, through the continuous contour line, will help to insure that your outline is subtly expressive of volume rather than mere delineation of a flat area. You will recall that in Form II (Chapter 4) we discussed the apparent edge or outline of objects of mass or space volume, and we insisted on drawing over the *surface* of the object rather than around the edge. The revolving contour line, of course, expresses the surface of the object. But for the purposes of this experiment, for which we want to visualize a changed form, an outline drawing will leave us freer to do this.

When these larger drawings have been made, study each of them and try to see a new and improved shape emerging from the basic form. The new shape should keep essentially, the over-all proportions of the first bottle, but should attempt to improve on it through changes in the swelling or narrowing of the volume, changes in the slopes of the surfaces, and so on.

Draw the new shape, which is suggested and inspired by the first, ordinary bottle, *inside* the existing bottle drawing (although in places the new design may protrude beyond these limits). Complete the experiment by filling in with black ink those parts of the old bottle not occupied by the new shape, as in Fig. 15-2.

Conclusions

After the experiment, you will realize how slight a change in shape will produce a radically different form, how easy it is to go too far and produce only a vulgar and ridiculous form. The refinement of form is a subtle process of addition or subtraction suggested by the visual imagination and one's aesthetic sensibility, as we discovered to be the case for pattern in Vision I (Chapter 14). In designing the new shape, you will have made both rational and instinctive decisions—decisions concerning the rhythm of part to part, the proportions of part to part, the structural authority of the new form, and so on. These judgments are part of your aesthetic response to form, and with them must come an awareness of how narrow are the limits of change that affect the aesthetic significance of form. The new shape that is "right" will be the shape that appears to have grown there on the paper; the glasses in Fig. 15-3 meet this criterion. The shape that appears most awkward and ill at ease is the one that has been the most forced or contrived.

The motive for this experiment has been the development of a theme, to help train your imagination to move from what *is* to what *might be*. This experiment assumes that a new bottle shape may be most successfully inspired by an examination of many existing bottles, both to provide a stimulus to the imagination and to set the train of images in motion. The ability to determine the "rightness" of shape is difficult to learn.[1] Natural aptitude for this helps, of course, but this method of starting with existing shapes should help to develop your imaginative and aesthetic awareness.

FIG. 15-1
Skeletal and contour-line structure of bottles.

FIG. 15-2
New shapes from old. The form of the new bottle can be seen clearly for comparative purposes against the black silhouette of the old. The new shapes may or may not be an improvement, but this ready comparison reveals how small are the limits by which the whole character of the original form may be changed.

FIG. 15-3

GLASSES

---

[1] "Rightness" of shape is invariably found in nature, and the artist is tuned to her rhythms. The student who wishes to learn about completeness of form must also look outward to the whole complex field of nature.

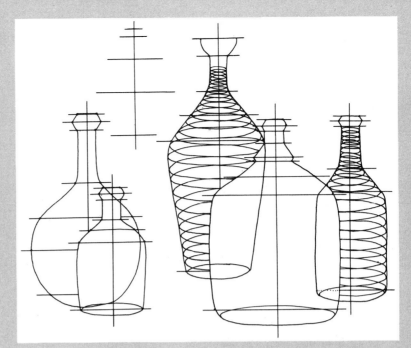

FIG. 15-1

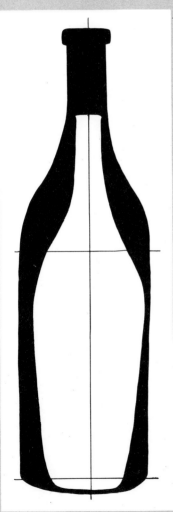

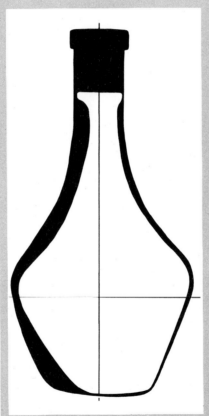

FIG. 15-2

FIG. 15-3

FIG. 16-1

16

pictorial

quality

What is it that moves a person to paint pictures? And what is it that imbues a good painting with a peculiar, magical life of its own which defies logical, cold-blooded analysis? These are big questions, and men have been asking them for a long time; they are worthy of more than the hints that are given in answer here. Yet an introductory hint must be given if this experiment in creating pictorial quality is to mean anything to the reader.

By "pictorial quality" we mean "an expressive and significant combination of shapes and colors." A painting springs from an urge to give expression to some aspect of experience which is affecting us powerfully, and the painter, through an expressive and significant use of shapes and colors, thus reveals his attitude to experience.

The second question is more difficult to answer—perhaps even defies answer—as the whole human capacity for imagination defies analysis, and paintings are the imagination given tangible form. Let us just say that any expressive and significant combination of shapes and colors has a strange power to affect us.

Shape and color in painting are significant in two ways. They affect our mood and suggest ideas. They strike at both the head and the heart. The painter, perhaps, has an advantage

FIG. 16-1

A significant and expressive arrangement of shapes and colors.

203

over the poet and the composer, at least initially, for human beings seem to respond more immediately to a thing seen than to words or sound, which take more time to absorb. The painter also has the advantage of color, which can so strongly affect the viewer, imparting joy or gloom, tranquillity or restlessness, excitement or passivity. Pictorial quality—color and shapes—exists, irrespective of the subject matter of the painting. An abstract or nonrepresentational painting may be totally without pictorial quality; so may a representational painting. On the other hand, both types of painting may possess it. Pictorial quality exists quite independently of the style of the painting, because people can respond to shape and color qua shape and color. We can react to these elements in themselves without having to consider what it is that has a particular shape or color: we can react to them in the abstract. And this response is largely intuitive; we do not have to stop to reason about how we feel about combinations of shapes and colors.

The aim of the following experiment will be to produce a nonobjective painting by free-drawing means. The painting will evolve through a series of mental and concrete images, each stimulating the production of a new image which can then be incorporated in the growing pictorial design. The finished painting may have pictorial quality; it may be "an expressive and significant arrangement of shapes and colors" —or it may not. That will depend on how effectively you are able to capture in concrete form the new images that suggest themselves in the exercise, using the unfamiliar mediums of wax and ink. Obviously, your instinctive response to shape and color will determine how significant and expressive are your images.

THE EXPERIMENT

This experiment will introduce the three basic colors—red, yellow, and blue—and the range of complementary colors that can be derived from them. To exploit this exercise fully, you should be prepared to learn by experience as you go along. The experiment is deliberately designed to keep you one step ahead in your response to the developing situation and to encourage you to make mental notes as results occur. As in much of the work of the previous sections, the value here lies not so much in the particular piece of work as in expanding the range of your aesthetic awareness and expression.

To supply the color for this painting, waterproof inks will be used because they are both intense in color and transparent; they are also quick-drying and extremely permanent. When a red waterproof ink is placed over a yellow one, the resulting color is a pure orange. Since the inks dry very fast and do not mix together, their transparency allows them to show through each other and thus produce an orange which is purer than that gained through normal mixing of pigments. For gaining a firsthand, practical knowledge about the basic colors and their derivatives, waterproof inks offer a much more efficient and exciting method than mixing pigments on a palette and then applying the new color to paper. In addition to the colored inks, we will introduce a resistant medium in this experiment— in this case, wax. The wax will resist the ink and thus render areas of the painting impervious to color. It will enable us to build up both shape and color in a way that could not be achieved by direct painting methods.

Two sheets of paper are required, each about 14″ x 16″ in size, one a sheet of newsprint and the other a good quality, smooth-surfaced white drawing paper. For the wax-resist, you can use an ordinary white wax candle. The best inks for this experiment are red (vermilion or crimson), blue (a light blue rather than a deep purple-blue), and yellow—the three basic colors from which, theoretically, all the others can be made. It is important to use the clearer reds and blues mentioned, because brown-reds and purple-blues do not work well when overlaying the other inks; they produce secondary hues that are muddy rather than clear and distinct.

To begin, cut or tear from an old newspaper a wide range of assorted shapes—just cut or tear quite freely as the inclination takes you, from long and thin shapes to fat and squat ones. When you have a good collection on hand, take the sheet of newsprint and glue a number of these cut and torn shapes onto it. Do this without too much conscious deliberation or selection, but keep an eye on the contrasting qualities of each shape selected, and place each where it would seem best to complement those around it. Some will overlap each other; some will be partially or completely isolated. When you feel that the sheet of newsprint is reasonably well covered, neither too crowded nor too empty, then stop. Each person will group his pieces differently, depending on his individual sense of the arrangement of the forms.

Although you will end up with an apparently meaningless jumble of newspaper shapes, they will finally embody a combination of shapes and colors which will grow through processes of addition and subtraction to an inevitable point of completeness.

For the second stage, you will need the sheet of good quality drawing paper. Make a pencil drawing of the design of the glued newspaper shapes. Do not draw merely the outline of the large figure, but include the overlapping lines of each individual paper piece. Once this is done, the first sheet is no longer required and can be thrown away. It has served its purpose by providing the free and nonobjective arrangement of shapes which you now have as a drawing. Now take the white wax candle and sharpen it down to a good drawing point (you will have to sharpen it quite frequently) so that it can do some intricate work. Approximately one-third of the total paper area has to be waxed over with the candle in this first step; and when you are considering where to wax, the spaces as well as the shapes should be considered. Distribute the wax regions fairly evenly over the whole paper area, applying the wax quite firmly, to close the grain of the paper. It is not necessary to follow closely the pencil outlines of the shapes or spaces; and if you want to, wax only a part of a shape or space. Since it is easier to develop secondary and tertiary colors by this overlay method, if we work from light hues to more intense hues, we will start with the yellow ink.

Using a large water-color brush loaded with ink, lay a rapid wash of yellow over the whole of the paper. Do this in a few quick actions and avoid the temptation to go back with the brush to touch up areas. Notice what happens with this first lay-in of color. The waxed portions, being resistant to the color, remain white, although parts take on a certain speckled quality where the wax did not completely close up the grain of the paper. The result is a yellow sheet of paper, with some white or speckled shapes, and it already suggests some emerging concrete images. It is at this stage that the basic character of the painting can be discerned. You are now in a position to sense the pictorial quality of the painting, as well as to deliberate on what should happen in the next stage of development.

The following steps become more complicated. New areas have to be protected by the wax-resist, and some of the areas first protected have to be scraped clear of wax. The reasons for these steps are fairly obvious. The wax that must be now applied over parts of the yellow area will protect the yellow shapes from the second color to be applied, namely, red. Areas of yellow that are not waxed will become orange; areas that are protected will remain yellow or yellow speckled with red. Scraping off some of the wax from the white or speckled parts will allow certain areas to become pure red. If all these whitish areas which were first protected were to remain waxed, then the red ink could not show up as its own pure color. Which parts of the yellow areas you protect and which areas you scrape off must be your decision. Only when the yellow ink is thoroughly dry and these second two operations are complete should the red ink be flooded over the whole of the paper. (On no account should any attempt be made to "paint in" specific areas or shapes; each color as it is applied must cover *all* the paper.)

After the application of the red ink, examine the design again to see what has happened. Where the red has gone over the yellow, there will be rich and luminous orange shapes. Where the yellow was waxed, pure yellow or yellow-speckled red will remain. The areas of white that were de-waxed will be pure red or red speckled with white. Where the white was left waxed from the beginning, white will remain, although by now it may be speckled with color. A great change has come over the painting with this application of the second color. The process of waxing and de-waxing has created secondary shapes that emerge only as the new inks, brushed over the surface, produce color changes. In fact, it is becoming obvious that you are really drawing with wax, although the results of the drawing appear only as the ink is brushed on. A coherent design is beginning to emerge, a design that has little in common with our first page of newspaper shapes.

Before applying the blue, study the painting closely, for the third color has the power to eliminate all the subtle colors and textures which are now present in the work. Since this color, too, is to be applied over the whole paper, you should try to imagine what effect it will produce. The orange will become brown, the red will become a rich violet, the yellow will be green, and the white will be blue. Blue is a potent colorizer; and of the three basic colors, it should be handled with the greatest care. If applied hastily, the blue can destroy much of the quality that has already been achieved. Therefore, the final layers of wax which are to repel the blue must be carefully applied; and any wax that is to be removed should be thoughtfully considered, so that when the blue is finally brushed over the whole painting, the colors change only where change is desired. Try to work in all the possible color changes somewhere on the painting, but remember that too many white areas are not desirable because they tend to break up the design.

After the blue ink is applied, a complete series of colors should appear: yellow, orange, red, brown, violet, green, and blue. Some of the areas will be speckled, and a few hybrid hues will probably show up. Note that only brown is a tertiary color, that is, a color produced from three sources.

But we are not quite at the end of the experiment. To see the true value of the colors (particularly any white regions), the subtlety of their gradations, and the more distinct outlines of the shapes, scrape the picture clean of wax with a razor blade. With the removal of the opaque film of wax, the whole painting should begin to glow. If you want to continue working on it, you can repeat the procedure with each color, or use other colored inks which are obtainable, to produce a considerable range of new hues. Or you might want to repeat only one color, to enrich the picture here and there.

Conclusions

Figure 16-1 provides a good illustration of pictorial quality. Only the combination of wax and transparent inks produces these special textures and distinctive color harmonies. In other words, some of the pictorial quality results from the natural properties of the materials used; a fact that is always true in painting, and one that makes it important to know your medium thoroughly. The painting produced in Fig. 16-1 is a remarkably homogenous composition. Both shapes and colors combine to form an expressive and rhythmic scheme. It is possible to see where and how the wax has acted as a "drawing" medium to determine a shape or a color area, and the disposition of the semi-white parts shows the artist's sensitivity to the problem of relieving the general redness of the picture. Notice that the yellow ink has all but disappeared (evidently it was not waxed to preserve it from subsequent inkings), and you might think this a deficiency in the work. On the other hand, more pure yellow might destroy the color and shape balance. In making this picture, the student had little conception of the finished result. There was no predetermined and final image toward which she was working. Instead, each stage of the process conditioned the next step and required a response from both the intuition and the intellect.

Figure 16-1 can be considered an effective painting (1) because all the colors in the painting were derived from the three primary colors and therefore possess a natural yet intriguing relationship to each other and (2) because the shapes originated freely and sequentially without being forced or contrived as a self-conscious "design"; they resulted from the gradual, deliberate build-up of color and the intuitive response of the artist to the emerging images. And they have power even though they do not "represent" any object or person.

Not all of your results will be this satisfactory, but in a second and a third painting, when you know more about the medium, you should be able to get an instinctive feeling for the process and have more control over the final outcome. In this exercise you do not have to worry about subject matter. You are free to experiment with pictorial quality in its purest sense. Many variations on this wax and ink method are possible: other colors in addition to the three primaries may be used, and more stages of waxing and de-waxing can be employed, all of which increase the possible number of shape and color combinations. The method can even be adapted to serve a strictly objective painting.

This experiment involving the three basic colors is a good introduction to secondary and tertiary hues, which emerge in the paintings. It should also surpass traditional study of the color wheel in giving you a better idea of how color works, of the nature of related families of color, and of opposite or complementary colors.

17

the

pictorial

imagination

We have seen that pictorial quality is an element that grows into the design of a drawing or painting that is intrinsically an organic part of its life, and that appears complete only in the finished work.

A painter usually pursues a direction that evolves from the first shape and the first color that appear on the canvas. He moves intuitively, identifying himself with the painting as it takes on a life of its own and carries him through a complex progression of stages to completion. The previous experiment attempted to reveal the authority of significant arrangements of form and color and the almost magical way they can take over the artist—dictate to him what he should do next. "Pictorial quality" suggests the independent authority of form and color over the artist, irrespective of subject matter or absence of it; pictorial quality affects the painter while he is actually working on the painting.

But what is it that impels him to work in the first place? We use the term "pictorial imagination" to mean the artist's capacity to recognize and to be stimulated by the aesthetic potential of something he sees or otherwise experiences (see Figs. 17-1 and 17-2) and his ability to create an image of greater power and significance in a pictorial context of shapes and colors. "Aesthetic recognition" as a part of pictorial imagi-

THE SLEEPING GYPSY (1897)
Henri Rousseau
Oil on canvas, 51 x 79 inches.
Here is a most mysterious
painting. It is the peculiar
quality of Rousseau's pictorial
imagination which renders
this strange vision.
(Collection, The Museum of
Modern Art, New York.
Gift of Mrs. Simon
Guggenheim)

211

nation, then, might be described as a capacity for heightened perception, which is one aspect of what we have called "vision." Not all artists possess a pictorial imagination. Many are illustrators or recorders of events, the counterparts of journalists in the literary arts.

We have seen how the English painter Graham Sutherland experienced a moment of heightened perception and subsequent vision when a bush of familiar thorns suddenly became terribly significant for him. The thorn painting (Fig. 14-2) is the result of a pictorial imagination, generous in its amount and brilliant in its ability to project new images into a pictorial context. There may sometimes be a long delay between the experience of heightened perception, the subsequent vision which projects images in the mind, and the physical act of creation. The nineteenth-century French painter Eugène Delacroix commented in his *Journal* that sometimes the memory of an object is sharper than the thing seen originally, for the image in the memory is the essential image, freed from irrelevant detail and distracting associations. Consequently, years later, the memory of a thing or an event may still motivate a work of art.

The question arises of whether a "pure" art exists, an art generated entirely from the subconscious resources of the artist, and of whether he need ever refer to visual objects for his inspiration; in other words, is the artist dependent on perception for the creative act? The answer must be left open. It is likely that even when an artist is working in a state of complete detachment and lucidity, divorced entirely from a sensory awareness of the world, the memory of some earlier perception is still the basic influence behind his design. But certainly in any introductory work in drawing and design, one must first attempt to increase one's powers of perception; at this stage, it is the best spur to pictorial imagination, and it is the surest way to accumulate bright, enduring images in the visual memory.

The following experiment attempts to stimulate your pictorial imagination by testing your ability to see things in strange graphic images and to transform these strange shapes into a drawing of imaginative expression.

FIG. 17-1

Large magnification of a tree root mass. What do the strange forms of this surface suggest to the pictorial imagination? Here is an image which must intrigue—but would you ever stop to look at an old root? (Photograph by Wayne Bitterman)

FIG. 17-2

Large magnification of a small patch of light made by hot sun on water. This detail is normally not visible to the naked eye. What forms do you see emerging here? The suggestions to the pictorial imagination may be principally of figures in fluid juxtaposition.

FIG. 17-1

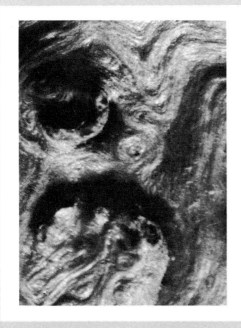

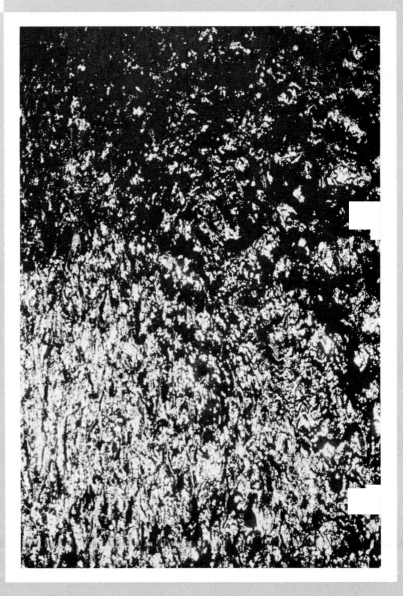

FIG. 17-2

THE EXPERIMENT

You will need a piece of string about 18 inches long, which will be used to make the first strange images. A sheet of white drawing paper not smaller than 22" x 15" is also needed. Now make a solution of black drawing ink or black water-color paint in a fairly shallow bowl; but do not dilute the strength of the black too much, or it will produce too pale and watery a mark. Spread some newspapers on the floor for protection and place the white drawing paper in the center. Immerse the string thoroughly in the black solution. On removing it from the bowl, squeeze it lightly to remove surplus liquid and then throw it down on the sheet of drawing paper.

When the string strikes the paper, it will recoil and twist and make a distinctive line or mark. Different types of string will make different kinds of lines and the manner in which the string is used will affect the mark produced. If the string is dropped rather than thrown, or if it is held at one end rather than rolled up in the palm, a different marking of the paper will result.

Once the first marks are on the paper, you may feel that the second throwing should be made with some deliberation, in such a way that it will create a certain relationship with the first mark. If so, this is all to the good. But for the purposes of this experiment, a series of random throwings of the string can be just as effective. When it is apparent that there are sufficient black lines and marks on the paper, that to add any more would confuse the "string drawing" already made, it is time to stop.

Now devote some time to scrutiny and contemplation of this complex pattern. Leave the "drawing" and then return to it, for too intense a scrutiny at one time will deaden rather than enliven your perception. The word "contemplation" suggests a relaxed and passive communion with the object or image, an attitude that is necessary here. After a while, definite shapes will emerge from the jumble of lines, shapes which start off ideas in the mind, stir the feelings, and suggest a new and more eloquent mental image. As you turn the paper around and upside down, you will see a variety of emerging forms, already partially set in a design or composition. The pictorial imagination must now take over. The goal is to realize these new images. Using a drawing pen and black ink, draw over and into the significant shapes that emerged from their background as you contemplated the string markings. Consciously exploit and pull out, through drawing, the new image your imagination has projected into them. But take pains to give some interrelationship to the forms in the drawing and to give the design an over-all spatial organization. The drawing, when complete, should be a homogeneous figure, since all the forms are developed from a common ancestor—the tracery of string marks.

It is interesting to note that when this experiment is performed by a group of students, roughly two-thirds will generally find objective representations in the patterns, such as figures in a landscape, fish beneath the sea, houses, trees, and so on. But here they will be drawn with far more vitality of line, far more expressive distortion, and with a stronger rhythmic movement than would be found in any normal drawing of the same subject matter. A higher degree of perception and imagination allows the other third of the group to find very personal forms in the string drawing (Fig. 17-3). These students will produce forms suggestive of the physical or emotional, or of such abstract concepts as "dignity" and "infinity."

Conclusions

Manipulating a string in this way is, of course, no serious substitute for the personal act of drawing. But it is a way of producing images for a direct stimulus to the pictorial imagination; and once experienced, stimulation will more readily occur in future situations. The capacity for vision, even of this elementary order, is a *sine qua non* for the artist. Without it he is merely a human camera. This experiment should have taxed your imagination and introduced you to the idea of metamorphosis in art. As Picasso has said, "A palm tree can become a horse. . . ."

215

Art operates on two levels: the genuinely creative and the merely derivative. The first tends to be a product of vision, and the second is a matter of reproducing an object or scene. The miracle of art lies in the artist's capacity for imaginative reaches of vision (see Fig. 17-4) and the hope is that the rest of us can keep up with him. William Blake, the nineteenth-century English visionary, once wrote: "He who does not imagine in stronger and better lineaments and in stronger and better light, than his perishing mortal eye can see, does not imagine at all."

Imagination is our most creative faculty. We all possess it to some degree, and we use it all the time. But we can all work to increase its effectiveness. Without it, we would have no sense of curiosity about the wonder of life, no speculative daydreams, and no creation in any of the arts.

FIG. 17-3

The development of a string drawing. The marks made by the string have almost disappeared in the over-drawing with the pen. Nevertheless, they were sufficient to engage the student's pictorial imagination for conscious development into this design. This is the sole purpose of initiating a configuration of lines and marks by means of string: to involve the student in further and more deliberate drawing.

FIG. 17-4

THE SLEEPING GYPSY

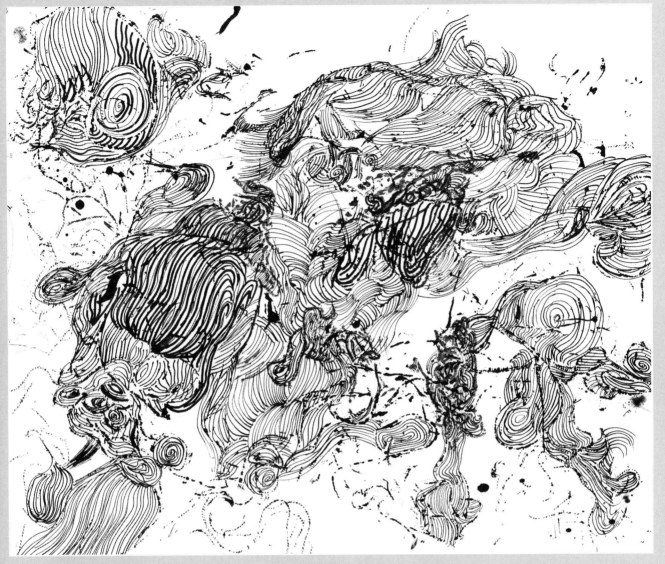

FIG. 17-3

FIG. 17-4

18

imaginative drawing from the model

Throughout this book we have stressed the importance of observation. Indeed, all of Part One was concerned with an objective and analytical inquiry into the nature of form and space. And drawing was the means by which we revealed the result of our inquiry.

As we have seen thus far in Part Two, the creative process is composed of three stages: perception, vision, and imaginative expression through some medium for giving form to vision. The experiment in this chapter unites these three factors in a drawing exercise. It requires acute observation of an object, going beyond an awareness of its external appearance; this demands perception. At the same time, it suggests certain ideas about the object which will provoke an imaginative attitude toward it; this involves vision. And then, through drawing, the object is transformed into a significant and expressive graphic image; here form is given to vision.

Since the model will be an object of volume and mass, the contour line could be used to reveal the underlying structure of the form. Also, since the object has a complex surface organization composed of planes and curved surfaces, points of thrust, and surface tensions, you might want to refer, for guidance, to the work carried out in Form V (Chapter 9). It is this dramatic quality of its surface which gives the object

LA SAINTE FACE
Georges Rouault
An arresting and compulsive image by one of France's greatest modern masters. The spontaneity of its execution suggests an almost simultaneous realization through drawing of the mental image. Here lies its graphic power. (Musée National d'Art Moderne, Paris)

219

some of the power that is its vitality and its fascination.

In this experiment, the object is the human head. To help stimulate your imagination, we will briefly discuss the type of personal character to be expressed in the new drawing. Late medieval writers often referred to the seven deadly sins of mankind: pride, avarice, lust, anger, gluttony, envy, and sloth. In the religious mystery plays of the Middle Ages, the actor portraying a particular sin would wear a mask that was shaped and painted to represent the sin. The mask was ordinarily semi-flat, to fit across the front of the face. However, the point of this exercise is not to design a mask, but to draw the head, to show the volume of the skull with its holes and bony projections. Nor should you concentrate on a likeness of the sitter. Rather, try to capture the structure of the head as an object of mass.

Select one of the seven deadly sins and let your imagination build up a facial image of it. What kind of a head conveys the idea of pride? Or of envy, or gluttony? As you draw from the model, try to adapt the natural form of the head to express your feelings toward the particular sin you have chosen, and portray your mental image of it. Your drawing should be meaningful as form (this is where the observation is necessary), and expressive of the sin (this is the imaginative element).

THE EXPERIMENT

A formally posed model is not necessary. Ask someone near you to hold his head in profile for a minute or so while you observe him. The profile is deliberately chosen because it aids perception of the structural elements of the head. Look intently at the profile and explore with your eye the movement of the planes and curved surfaces as they move over high points into valleys and along the ridges. More than likely you will find your eyes returning to one point, through which all the rhythms of movement seem to pass: the cheekbone, the high point where the bone of the skull pushes hard against the skin of the face. It reflects light and is a point of strong thrust that creates a surface tension on the skin stretched tightly over it.

There are two other main thrust points on the profile: the chin and the out-jutting frontal bone of the forehead above the eyebrow. The structure of the profile is organized around these three points of the skull. If you will recall the analogy we used in Form V (Chapter 9) to illustrate the proposition that surface planes and curves tend to be organized around a thrust force—the analogy of the cloth over the vertical pole—you will realize that the same thing is happening here over the surface of the face. If we carry this analogy further, we can compare the profile to a tent where the canvas is pulled tight around poles stuck in the ground. Where the canvas pulls against a pole, it changes its plane or direction. The form of the tent is determined by the positions of the poles; although they are not visible, you perceive they are there because of the surface tension of the canvas at the places where its surface changes direction. Our perception of the face and head works in very much the same way. From the surface tension of the skin and the change in surface direction, we learn something about the bony skull we cannot see. The eyes are in sockets or holes (we have done some drawing of holes earlier), while the rest of the profile is high ground or valley.

We are now beginning to go beyond appearances to a perception of the true structure of the head. One significant aspect of this experiment is the use of the contour line. If you will study Fig. 18-1, you will see that a strongly defined "flat" outline of the head does not appear. There is no dominant edge to the head; instead, the plane and curve just disappear beyond the line of sight, because no outline of the profile was drawn in the first place. The drawing was not started at the "edge," but was commenced within the form, at its most projecting point, the high point of the cheekbone.

Using the revolving contour line, draw the projection of the cheekbone, with the same technique you used to make the holes and projections of the wood form in Form II (Chapter 4). Now work *out* from this high point, allowing the pen or pencil to move rhythmically and to describe the planes and curved surfaces surrounding the cheekbone. Suggest the angle and direction of each plane—imaginatively feel it with your fingertips—and notice the rhythmic link these surfaces have with the chin and with the forehead. Each plane and curve can be seen, felt, and drawn as a separate contour region, yet all seem to revolve through and around the thrust points of the cheek, chin, and forehead. Like the canvas of a tent, the movements of the skin indicate the structure beneath. It is possible to draw this head without drawing an outline of any kind. As the line moves out from the cheekbone, exploring the various planes and curves, it stops automatically at the limits of the profile. In this way the mass of the head is realized through the drawing.

A glance at Figs. 18-1 and 18-2 will suffice to indicate how the characteristics of the sin have been expressed. The contour line has expressed the structure of the form, but the sin has been realized through imaginatively exploiting individual features: eyes, nose, and mouth, are specifically designed to reveal the feelings and mental images stimulated by envy and sloth. The features have then been arranged for the maximum of effect: eyes close together or far apart, deeply sunk or protruding, the mouth turning up or down, and the nose shown as beaklike or retroussé. Also, certain parts of the head have been distorted for expressive effect; bulging forehead and disappearing chin, for example. But all these imaginative treatments of the form have been heightened by the use of the contour line which has been adapted to express them.

Your drawing may well take two or three hours to make. The first drawings were made in pencil, with frequent reference to the model for information. These preliminary drawings were based principally on observation, although the contour line was used and the structural basis was derived from the three thrust points. The second drawings, which are those reproduced here, were made by reference to both the first drawings and the model. By then the artists were more confident and better able to give form to mental images without worrying too much about technique or form structure. Thus the head could take on its own imaginative existence as the epitome of the chosen sin.

Conclusions

All the important deductions from this experiment are really self-evident. A study of the drawings reproduced will yield some of them, even without reference to the text. But we should repeat the fundamental reason for making this drawing. It is to indicate that the creative process in the visual arts must integrate several seemingly independent factors. The first of these is sight itself, the process of observation. Second comes

FIG. 18-1

HEAD OF SLOTH
Imaginative drawing from the model.

perception, by which observation produces meaningful knowledge of the thing seen. Third is vision, through which this meaningful knowledge releases a whole range of imaginative ideas and mental imagery accompanied by intensified feeling. And finally we come to the means of expression—line, form, and color, disposed in space—without which, of course, the preceding stages can be nought.

This experiment has used all four of these stages. It has cheated a little because the imaginative idea about the head was injected verbally in the text and did not spring from perception of the object itself. One final point concerns the question of technique. Only when technique is not a conscious problem can the artist really work creatively. One of the values of using the contour line to express structure is that it enables the artist to depict volume and form by second nature, without thinking much about it. He is free to express his attitude, to know himself through drawing.

FIG. 18-2

HEAD OF ENVY
*Imaginative drawing from the
model.*

FIG. 18-3

LA SAINTE FACE

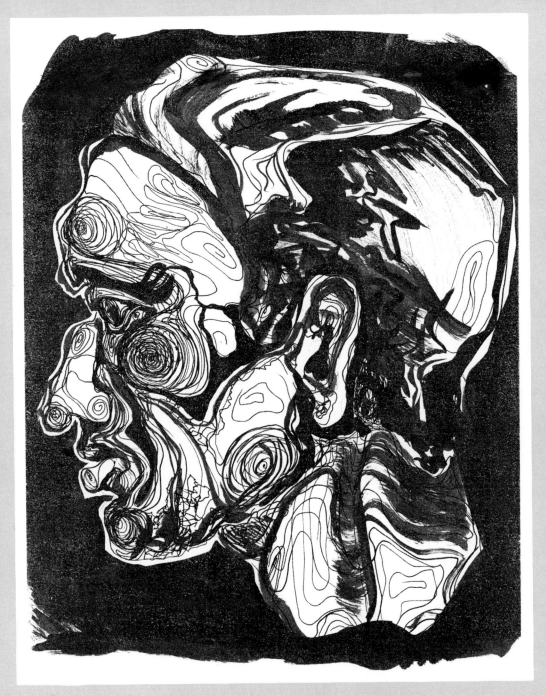

FIG. 18-2

FIG. 18-3

19

simultaneous observation and imagination

In this section, we will follow up the experiment in Vision V (Chapter 18) using the human head again as the subject, but this time with no verbal suggestion in the text to stimulate the imagination. The drawing medium also will be changed.

One of the principal conclusions reached after the last experiment was that a preoccupation with the technical difficulties of drawing or painting stifles the creative spontaneity that we associate with vision in art. Creative spontaneity is closely related to the developing process in art. Both are aspects of the visual imagination. The difference between them is simply one of time. Creative spontaneity refers to the immediate impulse to draw, to the first drawing, which sets the artist working and the sequence of images in motion: something he sees involves his imagination sufficiently for him to draw it and thus invest it with significance. The developing process, on the other hand, signifies the further development of this first drawing, step by step. As a sequence of events, creative spontaneity comes first, followed by the developing process, which is a building on to the graphic *image*, rather than the result of an immediate perception of the *object*.[1] This

AFRICAN DANCE MASK,
IVORY COAST
The simplified form given to the head in this mask is based on an awareness of the skull structure beneath the surface. The forehead, cheekbones, and chin become high points through which all the facial rhythms move.
(The American Museum of Natural History)

---

[1] In the work of the great artists, no such separation can be made. Creative spontaneity and the development of the image are fused, independent of time, in one inspirational act of expression.

227

experiment is concerned with creative spontaneity, with the quality of the immediate expression in a first drawing. Ask yourself why the drawings of young children about the age of five or six are so appealing. If you watch them drawing, you will see that they are not concerned with technical problems of representation and they have no self-conscious worries about whether others will understand or approve their drawing. The result has an urgent and vital quality because it is an immediate expression, stemming directly from the child's feelings and ideas about the object or the experience.

The purpose of the exercise proposed in this chapter is to help increase your capacity for creative spontaneity. Or to put it another way, it is to produce the conditions under which an immediate and unself-conscious response to an object or an experience can be made, a response or expression through drawing uninhibited by the technical problems of an academic approach.

But first we should explain what is meant by the title of this chapter, "Simultaneous Observation and Imagination." When we look at an object, we see not only its outward appearance but also its personal significance, and in that, we are using imagination. If you see a truck speeding toward you when you are crossing the street, you realize its potential danger and you move quickly out of its path. You have observed the appearance of the truck, but you have also had a significant realization of what would happen if you did not get out of the way. Or if you are thinking of buying some drinking glasses you may observe their shape, size, and color, but you also imagine yourself holding the glass and drinking from it. But the imagining need not be so utilitarian. The object can also take on symbolic significance. A piece of wood in the grass, for instance, could imaginatively become a snake. A drawing which is the immediate response to an object usually manages to combine the observed and the imaginative aspects of the object in a single, urgent expression; such a drawing possesses creative spontaneity.

The artist, by definition, has a highly developed imagination that enables him to visualize in an object many things that do not relate to its utilitarian possibilities. Such imaginative understanding, accompanied by strong feeling, is, as we have seen, of the nature of vision for the artist. He would tend to

FIG. 19-1

Monoprint of the observed head.

see the stick in the grass, for example, as a snake rather than as a club. For the layman, who is less sensitive visually than the artist, this simultaneous operation of seeing and imagining is at a less developed state. But if the layman, when making a drawing, could be as natural as a child—who more often than not has an artist's imagination—he, too, will unconsciously exploit a high degree of creative spontaneity and produce a drawing filled with the magic of art. As John Piper, the contemporary British painter (see Fig. 9-5), once remarked, "Child artists are the natural enemies of adult ones."

The head is a very significant object, expressive of all the qualities we associate with humankind—dignity, nobility, beauty, and on down the list. But it is also difficult to draw—another reason for choosing it as a model. Drawing the head is often given as an exercise in drawing skill, and the result is frequently academic, lifeless, and the very opposite of what we have called "creative spontaneity." In this experiment we will attempt to show how drawing the head can be transformed into a spontaneous and creative experience, for the layman as well as for the artist.

Earlier, we saw the inked surface of a glass plate as a sensitive medium for both tone and line drawing, from which a print can be pulled. Since this medium allows marks of drawing to be achieved rapidly and with ease, we will use it to overcome the technical difficulties that act as a barrier to creative spontaneity. The previous experiment focused our attention on the structure of the head and face and thus provided information about the object which will help you (the self-conscious adult) tackle this new drawing with freedom and surety.

THE EXPERIMENT

The head is a subtle structure of bony protuberances, planes, curves, and holes. This much we have already discovered. To sit down and make the customary pencil sketch of it may be a difficult and laborious task with a number of snares. If one does not observe the head as a whole, he may spend hours on one eye, trying to "get it right," without realizing that it needs the other eye to pull it into its context. The novice draws every-

FIG. 19-2

Monoprint of the observed head.

thing he sees quite separately, and the head becomes a life-less mask, a collection of parts.

In the last exercise (see Figs. 18-1 and 18-2), we found that the three high points of the head—through which all the surfaces, planes, and curves move and which are the structural bases for the form—are the chin, cheekbone, and forehead. Using the contour line, it was impossible to be sidetracked by all the details of the face: the eye sat simply in its hollow socket, the nose was a projecting plane, and the mouth fitted into the contour line's organization of the surface of the face.

Similarly, the inked surface of the glass plate does not allow preoccupation with individual features. The ink dries fairly rapidly, and one cannot see very much of what is happening on the plate, so there is no stopping to make constant comparisons with the model and no worrying because the drawing does not "look right."

Drawing the head on the glass plate demands an immediate reaction to the object. What goes down there is a "first seen" quality—the result of the immediate impulse to draw—without fussy drawing of representational details. It is useful to work in pairs for this experiment, with one person modeling and one drawing. Ink the glass plate and assemble all the tools previously found useful for drawing in the ink. (A piece of rag for wiping off ink, to make strong white parts in the drawing, is a necessity for this experiment.)

The plate is ready, and the head is before you. You have about half an hour to work on the glass before the ink becomes too dry. Start by wiping off the ink to give the high point of the cheekbone, and then do the same for the chin and the forehead, allowing the highly fluid quality of the medium its own freedom of movement. Work rapidly, taking a look at the head and then moving directly into the ink: scrape, brush, scratch, and wipe.

In conclusion, we will let the illustrations speak for themselves. Four heads drawn in the manner described above are reproduced in Figs. 19-1 to 19-4. Each of these drawings is a simple statement of essentials. There is a minimum of detail and an emphasis on the broad masses of light and dark or, rather, the high points and the depressions (see Fig. 19-5). The forehead, cheekbone, and chin dominate the drawings. The eyes sit in their inky sockets: and where the artist has felt

FIG. 19-3

Monoprint of the observed head.

the need for some linear definition, as in the eyelids of Fig. 19-4, a sharp tool has drawn for a moment in the ink.

After this direct approach for so short a time, the glass gives little indication of the drawing made in the ink. The print, when taken, is quite a shock. The head that emerges is bold in form and vital and convincing as drawing. It is full of life and drama. In it, in fact, observation and imagination have simultaneously produced a drawing of creative spontaneity. When you study your print, think of the pencil drawing you might have made of this head.

FIG. 19-4

Monoprint of the observed head.

FIG. 19-5

AFRICAN DANCE MASK

FIG. 19-4

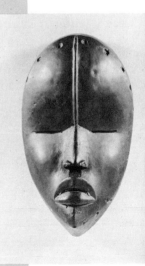

FIG. 19-5

20

looking with intent:
simultaneous aspects
of objects

VIOLIN AND GRAPES (1912)
Pablo Picasso
*An illustration in the late
Cubist style of fragmentation
of the object, which inevi-
tably occurs when the artist
is concerned with revealing
several aspects of the form or
revealing structural essentials.
(Collection, The Museum of
Modern Art, New York.
Mrs. David M. Levy Bequest)*

The phrase "looking with intent" was used in Part One to suggest that there are degrees of looking, the most common of
which is to look at a thing vaguely, merely for purposes of
identification, or even just to avoid falling over it. But when
we are looking intently, identification is a secondary goal, for
we are interested; we are curious to discover all we can, visually, about the object. We also experience what was described
in the previous chapter as the simultaneous operation of the
imagination. The eye, physically, takes in all it can see, while
the imagination speculates on unseen aspects of the object.

What are these "other aspects" of an object? They fall into
two categories. There are those that cannot be seen from one
particular viewing position, but which we know about through
having seen them on other occasions from a different position
(the other side of the object, for example). Secondly, there
are those that cannot be seen from an external viewing position: the hidden, internal aspects of the object. We must dissect the object in order to project images of these aspects. In
the case of some objects, we can actually physically dissect
them and reveal their internal prospect (see Fig. 20-1), and
this view can later, when we look at the exterior of the object,
be conjured up by the mind's eye. Take a tomato, for instance.
Externally, it is round and red. But if you slice up enough

237

tomatoes, you will become so familiar with their inside sectional appearance that you will never see a tomato without also visualizing its cross section. Many forms and objects, however, cannot be easily dissected. Our imagination has to act like a surgeon's knife and cut through the object to reveal those hidden places of which we have no sensory knowledge.

This kind of X-ray approach, which leads inevitably to the fragmentation of the object, has been one of the major interests of modern painting during this century. The early cubist style of Pablo Picasso and Georges Braque in 1908-1909 imposed the artist's structural geometry on the natural form of the object. When this structural fragmentation was allied to a paint surface of arbitrary tonal planes, the breakdown of the natural form was complete. Eventually, paintings were built up by such "fragmented masonry" without the painter having recourse to any visual subject matter. The form was developed imaginatively, to take on its own life (see Chapter 16, Vision III, "Pictorial quality").

Later phases of cubism introduced the practice of depicting not only what can be *seen* of an object, but also what is *known* about the object, all in one painting. This, of course, produced many difficulties for the viewer, who had been conditioned for so many centuries to an art concerned only with the appearance of things seen from one viewpoint. "Simultaneous projection" in art, the cubist invention of combining differing aspects of the figure or object in the same composition, thus projecting them simultaneously, produced paintings of the head, for example, with a profile superimposed over a full face. Picasso's "Violin and Grapes" (Fig. 20-2) treats the subject matter in the same way. The painter shows us the full face and the profile of the instrument, together with several other aspects of the object. Such an imaginative break-up of the forms will obviously reveal more about the subject than the traditional single-viewpoint representation. It is like getting several paintings for the price of one!

The following experiment will introduce you to the many differing aspects of apparently simple objects. Its primary purpose is to initiate the habit of looking with intent, to instill an awareness of the unseen, to take you once more to the brink of nonobjective art by yet another path. The work will be carried out in three parts. First, through a series of experi-

FIG. 20-1

Cross section of the lily seed pod revealing aspects of the form difficult to imagine from merely external appearances.

FIG. 20-2

VIOLIN AND GRAPES

FIG. 20-1

FIG. 20-2

mental drawings you will imaginatively reveal different exposures of three simple geometric figures. At some stage, a symbol of the object should emerge. Then will follow a series of internal "aspect drawings" made after physically cutting into a fruit. Finally, you will be asked to translate one series of drawings into a composite pictorial design, by projecting simultaneously all the discovered exposures of the object.

THE EXPERIMENTS

Make a cone, a cylinder, and a solid triangle of stiff paper. They do not need to be very accurate or very large—about 6 inches high is large enough to serve as models which can be imaginatively broken down through drawing. Made from paper, they are, of course, hollow; the model is a defined region of space rather than a solid form. As we pointed out in Form II (Chapter 4), volume has this dual role.

In this experiment, the two roles of volume are interchangeable. There is no need to make a base for these figures, since you will need to pick them up and look inside. The first step is to make a series of small drawings of each figure. First, make a straightforward drawing of the model as it appears at the normal eye level. Place this in the top left corner of the sheet of paper, then produce a series of 2-inch squares to the right side of it and beneath in orderly rows. You may need between ten to twenty squares.

The goal is to draw as many different aspects of the paper model as you possibly can. Figures 20-3 and 20-4 are the drawing responses made to this exercise by several students. How are such responses achieved? First, by viewing the object from many different positions and drawing each new observation. This is easy to do, for the model can be picked up and held at many angles and in many positions. Three or four drawings made in this way are sufficient. The drawings which follow are more difficult. For now you are asked to draw not just what you *see* but what your eye and imagination together can reveal. Try to visualize the object cut through and opened out. Imaginative fragmentation of the model is not easy, particularly if the fragment when drawn is to retain its identity as part of a cone, or a cylinder, or a solid triangle. A study of Figs. 20-3 and 20-4 will indicate the many forms that visual-

FIG. 20-3

Drawings exploring the aspects of a cone.

FIG. 20-4

Drawings exploring the aspects of a cylinder.

FIG. 20-3

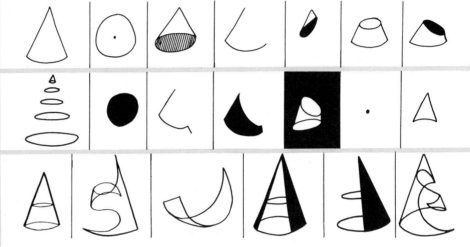

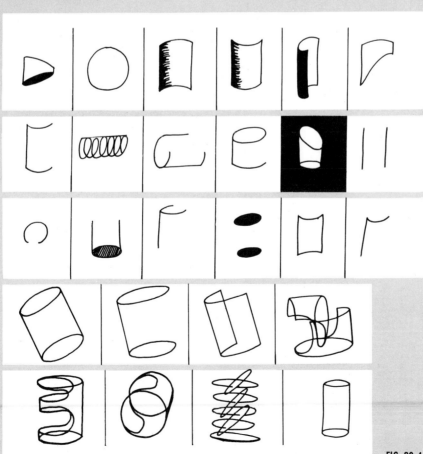

FIG. 20-4

imaginative fragmentation can take. Some of the drawings can be taken as aspects of a solid figure; others are regions of space, partly defined by a shell—such is the imaginative interchangeability between solid form and defined space, to which we previously referred in Form II (Chapter 4). Again, some of these drawings become so simple as linear symbols of the object that they are almost a form of "writing."

Eventually, you will have exhausted the aspect possibilities of this particular object. Some people may have only seven or eight drawings, others as many as twenty. When you have completed the drawings of all three objects, select one drawing from each series which in your opinion is the simplest in terms of drawing, yet which also has the strongest power to suggest the likeness or the idea of the original model. If you have made such a drawing, it could be termed a symbol of the object. A visual symbol must possess strong communicative power; therefore it must be simple, and it must be abstracted from the original object. All the aspects you have made of the three objects are also abstractions of the objects. It follows from this that such an abstraction can possess symbolic power.

The second part of this experiment consists of making drawings similar to those just completed. But, now, instead of *imaginatively* cutting through the object, we shall actually cut it with a knife. Use some kind of fruit, such as a lemon or a tomato. This series of drawings should be set out on a single sheet of paper exactly like the others, with a simple drawing of the whole fruit made in the top lefthand corner. Now, proceed to cut up the model, making a drawing of each new aspect as it is revealed through the surgical operation. You will no doubt find this series of drawings easier to make, for now your imagination is reinforced by a physical reality which can be seen and handled. Figure 20-5 is an illustration based on cutting a lemon. These aspects of lemon are also abstractions of lemon, and at least one drawing could be used as a symbol of lemon.

The final work of this section touches once more on pictorial quality, at least on the part of pictorial quality which has been defined as an "expressive and significant use of shapes." Select one of the sheets of drawings which you have just made, either the aspects of the cone, cylinder, solid triangle, or fruit. You will no doubt select the drawings most successful in revealing interesting and different presentations of the model. The proposition

FIG. 20-5

Drawings revealing the discovered aspects of a lemon.

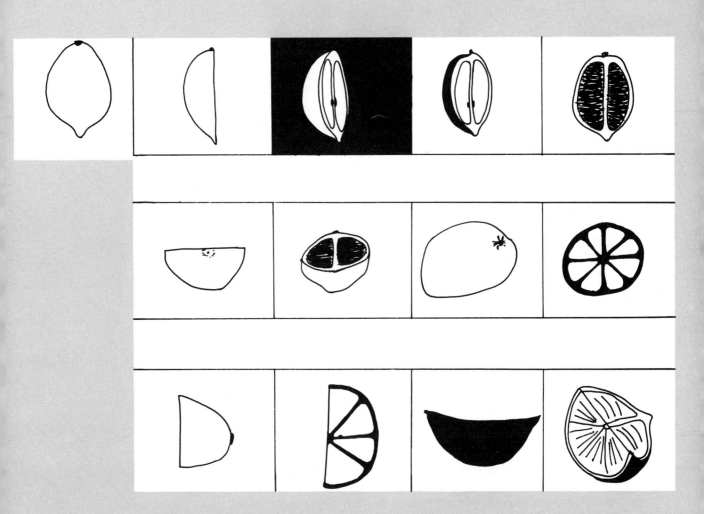

now is to take all aspect drawings of this one particular model and organize them into one pictorial design. You may fit as many as twelve or fifteen aspects into some kind of pictorial organization within a square or rectangular area. A convenient size for the area would be approximately 8″ x 8″. Make the drawing entirely in black and white. Figures 20-6 and 20-7 show two such drawings. Figure 20-7 makes use of solid black against textured white and gray, achieved with a wax-resist. Figure 20-6, however, makes use of tones or washed-in dilutions of ink to achieve the grays. In both of these illustrations, the differing aspects of the one object are projected simultaneously into the picture area to make an expressive and significant organization of shapes. Figure 20-7 is formed from the aspects of the solid triangle; Fig. 20-6 from aspects of the cone.

Conclusions

Now we can see that if new and unfamiliar exposures of an object are revealed when we look with intent, the act of drawing aids such visual, imaginative exploration and, at the same time, fixes and makes permanent the image of the new aspect. Without the drawing, no permanent visual sign or symbol of the discovery remains, either to provide a graphic image for any imaginative development or to elicit a direct response per se.

As you regard Figs. 20-6 and 20-7, one important question should be asked. Could these pictorial designs have been achieved as effectively by a deliberate drawing of a "set" subject, say a pictorial presentation of lemons, or triangles? From the author's experience with his own students, his answer would be "No." Left to your own devices with such a subject, it is more than likely that you would have concentrated in building up a formal composition, say of lemons, as they would appear from one viewpoint, rather than considering their hidden aspects as potential shapes for pictorial design. There is no doubt that the three drawings illustrated have benefited compositionally from all our previous work on structure and on the organization of space. In fact, because of our earlier study, we do not need a set experiment dealing with "composition." Composition involves simply the manipulation of space and a structural significance given to form, and these are things we have been dealing with right from the beginning. The importance of these final drawings, within the context of this chapter,

FIG. 20-6

Aspects of the cone simultaneously projected in a drawing achieving pictorial quality.

FIG. 20-7

Aspects of the solid triangle simultaneously projected in a drawing achieving pictorial quality.

FIG. 20-6

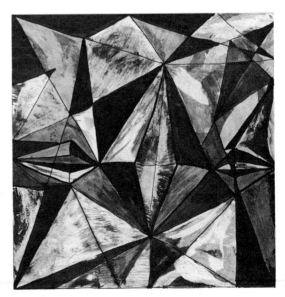

FIG. 20-7

lies in their authentic exposition of a single object. They are both convincing and revealing as studies of "cone-ness" or "triangle-ness." They go beyond a representation of external appearances to show the greater reality of the object's total nature. And although they are nearly abstract, the link connecting them to an act of perception—to looking with intent—may still be recognized.

For the beginning student, the perceptive act is an important factor. He should be able to take the thing seen and consider its total nature, its many aspects rather than recognize merely its external characteristics. Art is not imitative reproduction, or a kind of pretty picture-making, or a purely mechanical exercise of pattern-making. Art is an attitude to life and the things of life; it is an awareness of the structural and organic rhythms of the universe, visually expressed. This is the kind of commitment an artist, and a student of art, must have. It is a commitment to reveal (from a position of inquiry and personal attitude) rather than to imitate. The final works of this chapter should be the result of such an attitude, which is initiated by looking with intent, sustained by inquiry and an increased power of perception, developed by reason, and accompanied by a heightened emotional urge. These elements are synthesized in the two drawings previously mentioned.

Free drawing to find a symbol

By now, you should realize that the ways of drawing can be as varied as the ways of writing a letter, and just as personal. We have seen that the quality of a drawing is not based primarily on the amount of time or sweat put into it—or even on the skill applied. Instead, it depends on how intently the artist has looked at things, and how rich his imagination has been in creating images that carry him beyond mere visual reality or appearances. Any markings made in any medium to record the image, we have called "drawing." How much of this concept will have been assimilated by a person reading and drawing his way through this book cannot be easily assessed. It is probably better if comprehension exists at a subconscious level, for too conscious a striving to attain it destroys spontaneity of vision, so necessary to art.

With all this in mind, a group of students were given a deliberately vague briefing and then left entirely alone. The

FIG. 20-8

Quick studies from observation of the eye.

intention was to follow up the work in Chapter 20 but without any rigid terms of reference. They were asked to pick an object and then reduce it to a symbol through drawing. The symbol was then to be used freely and imaginatively as the motif for the cutting of a linoleum block. Two or three students chose the human eye as their object, and it is their work which illustrates this concluding experiment. First they made some drawings directly from the eye, but with a boldness and vigor that indicates their freedom from worry about technical means (they all used a different medium). It was as if the previous work had released inhibitions about "drawing," enabling them to concentrate on more expressive aspects of the eye.

Figure 20-8 is typical of the first drawings executed with pen, brush, and finger—in ink, pencil, and even monoprint. The treatment of one of these drawings is derived from those rapid sketches of twigs made in Drawing Marks I (Chapter 2). But none of them are characterized by that hesitant groping after irrelevant linear detail which enfeebles beginning drawing.

To simplify the first drawing was the next task. Without prompting, the students executed many small, rapid sketches of various aspects of the eyes, breaking down the first drawing. Each sketch was a graphic image in its own right, and each suggested the degree of simplification required to produce the next drawing. The final drawing produced a concrete image of "eye-ness," to which, in the student's opinion, nothing could be added or subtracted without detriment to the symbol that had emerged. Figure 20-9 shows seven such sketches culminating in a subtle and refined symbol abstraction in the shape of a scroll. This final drawing is a monoprint taken from the glass plate. These seven drawings make use of a cunning interchange of black and white. In drawing number 3, the white space in the center of the eye becomes the black eyeball in drawing number 4, thus clarifying the earlier confusion in this part of the drawing.

These drawings represent the "developing idea" in action once more. When we look at Fig. 20-9, we wonder if drawing number 7 could have been achieved directly from the first eye drawing without the six stages of transition. Probably not. Nor is there much doubt that the enthusiasm and comparative ease with which these drawings were produced came partly from the student's ability to "look with intent," to

FIG. 20-9

Seven drawings illustrating the step-by-step reduction of the eye drawing to its final abstract symbol.

1

2

3

4

5

6

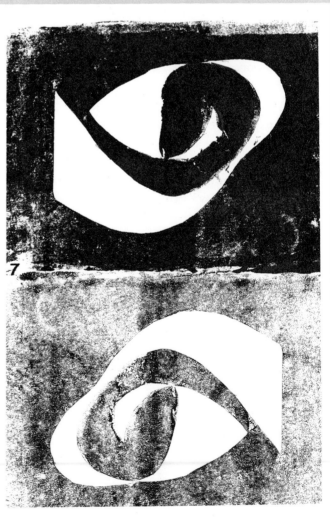

7

discover aspects of objects that otherwise would have been passed over.

When the eye was finally reduced by drawing to a symbol, a symbol that lacked none of the essential qualities of eye but that had added a certain mysterious unintelligibility [1] to the idea of "eye-ness," the final project could be started. The only instruction given to the group at this point referred them back to the linoleum block prints made in Vision I (Chapter 14) and suggested that study of these would indicate good balances of black and white, of line to area, and so on. The problem then was to transfer the eye symbol to the surface of a large block of linoleum. Figure 20-10 illustrates one of the results. In this design, the eye motif is still visible, although in translating the drawing to the block the eye could easily enough have been lost through the expansion of the motif the problem demands. This is an intelligent and pleasing use of the motif. Vital in movement and rhythm, with space and form convincingly integrated through the organic sweep of linear patterns, the design is complete as it stands.

One of the most difficult things to develop is the ability to see a shape or an image in more than one context. For example, a twig with its bud might well become the model for a concrete street lamp, or as we have already seen in Form V (Chapter 9), a crumpled piece of paper can become a mountainside. The students performing the concluding exercise experienced less difficulty in this regard than do most beginners. They moved from the observed object to imaginative abstractions in drawing, and on to the changes in the motif necessitated by engraving a block, without the usual awkward and tentative transitions. They readily jumped from medium to medium to give expression to their ideas and were not overly worried about "how to draw." Their understanding that there are many aspects of reality, their willingness to probe beyond mere appearances, their realization that they, themselves, possess attitudes about things, and that these are spontaneously expressible—all this contributed to their freedom.

No doubt artists are still born and not made. But even the nonprofessional artist may aspire to creative rather than imitative levels of performance.

FIG. 20-10

Linoleum block design based on the abstract eye motif.

---

[1] See Space III (Chapter 7) for Sir Herbert Read's statement concerning the symbol and "unintelligibility."

REVIEW

Vision I

Building up a nonobjective design through addition and subtraction can be carried out without using the linoleum block.

1. Scratchboard can be used by scraping out a white shape first, putting part of it back with brush and ink, scraping out again and then inking back, until, by this give-and-take method, the area is eventually occupied by some arrangement of black and white forms.

2. On a white sheet of paper, using two brushes—one for white paint and one for black—build up forms. First add free black forms, then modify them by breaking into them with white paint. Continue this process of alternate addition and subtraction until the design is complete.

3. Work as in 2 above, with charcoal and kneaded eraser. Use the charcoal to lay in areas of black quite freely on the paper and use the eraser actually as a drawing tool, to take off in the black regions. Build up until the design is complete.

Vision II

The following experiments are suggested to develop a stronger realization of common qualities of "shapeness" between forms and of how small a change in form is required to produce a new aesthetic implication.

253

1. Draw freely with a brush and ink on a large sheet of paper to discover the transitions by which a square becomes a circle. Brush in a solid square at the top left, and working to the right, repeat this square, but make one change in its shape on each occasion. For example, the second square might lose a corner, the third another corner, and so on, until a complete circle results. Repeat this by going from cylinder to cone, square to triangle, etc. Notice the intermediate stages and realize how basically "near" each other are these forms. Try this shape metamorphosis by brush drawing transitions from free forms, and see what shapes result.

2. Using two illustrations from this book for references, the Greek amphora (Fig. 8-17), and the wine glasses (Fig. 15-3), make a series of drawings of each object, each drawing attempting to exploit further the most personally attractive aspect of the original. The aspect might be the object's curvature, or its slim proportion, or its angularity. How far can this expressive change go before it degenerates into caricature or vulgar exaggeration and novelty? Is the original object already at a point of maximum aesthetic expression?

3. Change unitary form into compound form. In a rectangle about 9″ x 7″, brush in a solid black circle occupying approximately one-fifth of the total area. Using the brush, extend this figure into the remaining area of the rectangle by pulling out limbs, protrusions, etc. Stop when the new form is sufficiently complex and when the empty area is satisfactorily occupied. This extension process can be done with many different types of unitary form.

Vision III

Sensitivity to pictorial quality is most effectively induced by a personal involvement with shape and with color, an involvement demanding value judgments of a personal nature. Here are two suggestions for work in this chapter.

1. Try abstracting from great paintings. Select some prints of paintings by El Greco, Rubens, Titian, Raphael, or other great artists (magazine reproductions are quite suitable for this). Pick out the main forms of the design and the main rhythms which hold the design together.

Attempt to express these forms and these rhythms in a black water-color drawing with a full range of tones, one which will be an expressive abstract of the original.

2. Collect a whole range of possible collage material centered around a specific color range—reds to browns or blues to greens—and consider textures and forms as well as color. Select from a wide range of sources. Assemble a design using this material, bearing in mind the phrase, "a significant and expressive combination of shapes and colors." Remember the complementary function of black and white to color. When the assemblage is complete, varnish it. This will give a homogenous quality to the color and the forms of the design.

Vision IV

A constant exercise of the imagination must always be sought in art. The following work is suggested as an appendage to the chapter on the pictorial imagination.

1. Select some large, full-page black-and-white photographs from books or magazines and using four pieces of paper, mask out areas of the picture, thus allowing concentration on one small region. After some experimentation, select one such region and enlarge it into a black-and-white drawing which will almost certainly be abstract, and which may possess its own strong pictorial quality.

2. Spatter some blots, large and small, onto a sheet of drawing paper. What do they suggest? How would you draw into them? Will the finished drawing suggest a landscape or a figure? Find some reproductions of "blot drawings" made by Alexander Cozens, the English eighteenth-century landscape painter.

3. Observe surfaces in nature, stained and molded surfaces of rocks, leaves, tree bark, and similar things. What suggestions of forms are to be found in these variegated surfaces; what do they suggest to the pictorial imagination? Draw!

4. Observe some highly magnified illustrations of biological cross sections. Here is a complete new world of form. Once again, what will the pictorial imagination find here? Make more drawings.

Vision V

For further imaginative drawing from the observed object:

1. From the figure, make a dozen quick drawings of diverse, five-minute poses by the model. Place the figures thus drawn in a new imaginative context in one design. It will be a help to study some of the figure compositions of Nicolas Poussin, the seventeenth-century French artist.

2. From nature, draw a cabbage. Transform this into a face of old, old age.

3. Set up some drapery, three or four separate lengths, having varied organizations of folds, in vertical formation against a wall. Keep about three feet of space between each length. Draw these vertical lengths of cloth using wide paper, and fill in the gaps by introducing an imaginary *draped* figure. This figure should not intrude, but should belong naturally among the folded material and result in an extravaganza of figure and fold.

Vision VI

Many variations can be made in monoprint technique, and they are worth developing; for as a drawing medium allowing the immediate expression of an image or an idea, the monoprint cannot be surpassed. If a drop or two of glycerine is added to the ink, this will retard drying and thus allow more time for drawing and modeling in the ink. Celluloid and plastic may be used instead of glass as the printing surface, and some strange results will occur by printing on experimental papers or materials. The medium is as valuable for free imaginative drawing as for drawing a variety of observed objects.

Vision VII

Further experiments in the breakdown of the object and the revelation of its several aspects in one composite design should be carried out in several different drawing mediums. The subject matter can extend from the natural object to the mechanical one. (Think of the aspects of an engine cylinder block, for example, as a subject for a composite design involving simultaneous projection.) It is also possible to move from the single object to the group, which presents imaginative and organizational problems of some magnitude. Development of the chapter in this way challenges one's creative and technical resources.

index